G000091320

Education in Developing Asia

Volume 1

Education and National Development:

Priorities, Policies, and Planning

Don Adams

Asian Development Bank
Comparative Education Research Centre
The University of Hong Kong

© 2002 Asian Development Bank

Jointly published by:

Asian Development Bank
6 ADB Avenue
Mandaluyong City
P.O. Box 789
0980 Manila
Philippines

Fax: (632) 636 2444
E-mail: adbpub@adb.org

and

Comparative Education Research Centre
The University of Hong Kong
Pokfulam Road
Hong Kong, China

Fax: (852) 2517 4737
E-mail: cerc@hkusub.hku.hk

Obtainable from either address.

Series: Education in Developing Asia
Series editor: Mark Bray

Layout and index by Sara Wong.

The findings, interpretation, and conclusions expressed in this study are entirely those of the author and should not be attributed in any manner to the Asian Development Bank or the University of Hong Kong.

A summary of an earlier version of this booklet was presented as an article in Vol.29, No.7 (1998) of the International Journal of Educational Research, published by Pergamon Press. The publishers of this booklet thank Pergamon Press for permission to reproduce some of the materials from the journal article.

ISBN 971-561-403-5
ADB Publication Stock No. 100301

The series

Education in Developing Asia

has five volumes:

1. Don Adams (2002): *Education and National Development: Priorities, Policies, and Planning*;
2. David Chapman (2002): *Management and Efficiency in Education: Goals and Strategies*;
3. Mark Bray (2002): *The Costs and Financing of Education: Trends and Policy Implications*;
4. W.O. Lee (2002): *Equity and Access to Education: Themes, Tensions, and Policies*; and
5. David Chapman and Don Adams (2002): *The Quality of Education: Dimensions and Strategies*.

Series Editor:

Mark Bray

Contents

List of Tables   iii
Figure   iii
List of Boxes   iii
List of Abbreviations   iv
Foreword   v

Introduction   1

The Regional Context   3
Demographic Changes   3
Economic Changes   6
Social Changes   9
Education Development   11
A Typology of Developing Member Countries   15

Education, Economic Growth, and Social Change   20
Education and Economic Growth   20
Education and Poverty Reduction   24
Education, Social Change, and Social Cohesion   25
Teaching and Learning: Inside the Black Box   27
Policies, Issues, and Trends by Subsystem   33
   Preprimary Education   34
   Basic Education   34
   Junior Secondary Education   36
   Senior Secondary Education   36
   Tertiary Education   37

The Changing Pattern of Policy and Planning   39
Decentralization and Localization   39
   The PRC Case   42
   The India Case   45
Achievements, Risks, and Problems   47
Planning and Sustaining Decentralized Education Changes   50
Improving School-Community Relations   52

Emerging Education Trends and Strategies   55
Education Governance and Management   55
   Policy 1. Strengthening of Institutional Infrastructure in the Center   56
   Policy 2. Improving Education Planning and Policy
   Capabilities of Provincial and District Institutions   57
   Policy 3. Restructuring School-Level Management   58
   Policy 4. Regional Research and Training Role for ADB   59

Developing and Sustaining High-Quality, Equitable, and
Adequately Financed Education Systems 59
    Policy 1. Developing Effective Basic Education 60
    Policy 2. Developing Effective Secondary Education 62
    Policy 3. Developing Effective Tertiary Education 63
Developing Better Indicators and Information 64
    *Policy 1. Strengthening the Policy Relevance of a Regional
    System of Education Indicators* 65

Developing More Effective International Assistance **66**
    *Strategy 1. Improving Operational Coordination between
    ADB and DMC Governments* 66
    Strategy 2. Monitoring Program and Project Implementation 67
    Strategy 3. Improving Program and Project Sustainability 68
    *Strategy 4. Continuing Dialogue on Long-Term Dangers of
    Extensive ADB Assistance* 69

Conclusion **71**
Note on the Author 73
References 74
Appendix 77
Index 79

List of Tables

Table 1: Regional Comparisons of Human Development, 1997   3
Table 2: Selected Demographic Conditions   4
Table 3: Economic and Social Conditions   7
Table 4: NIEs and South Asia Comparison   9
Table 5: Gross Enrollment Rates by Education Level, 1975-2010   12
Table 6: Total Regional Public Education Expenditure   14
Table 7: DMC Groupings   16
Table 8: Adult Illiteracy Rates, 1995   18
Table 9: Mid-Year Population, 1995   18
Table 10: GDP per Capita Annual Growth Rates, 1985-1995   21
Table 11: Selected Studies of School Effects in Asian Economies   29
Table 12: Dimensions of Effective Schooling   31
Table 13: Four Basic Stages of Agricultural Productivity
    and their Learning Requirements   37
Table 14: Cross-Country Comparisons of Education Decentralization   40
Table 15: Responsibility of Panchayati Raj Institutions for
    Primary Education, Various Three-Tier Indian States, 1995   46
Table 16: Models of School and Community in the Provision of Education   53
Table 17: How Involvement of the Community Can Improve Education   54

Figure

Figure: Total Regional Public Education Expenditure   13

List of Boxes

Box 1: Case of Inconsistent Data – Nepal   16
Box 2: Integrated Early Education and Development – The Philippines   35
Box 3: Inequities Resulting from Decentralization – The PRC   44
Box 4: The Panchayati Raj Initiative – India   45
Box 5: Mobilizing Local Participation – Pakistan   49

List of Abbreviations

ADB	—	Asian Development Bank
DMC	—	Developing Member Country
GDI	—	Gender-related Development Index
GDP	—	Gross Domestic Product
GER	—	Gross Enrollment Rate
GNP	—	Gross National Product
HDI	—	Human Development Index
HPI	—	Human Poverty Index
Lao PDR	—	Lao People's Democratic Republic
NIE	—	Newly Industrialized Economy
NGO	—	Nongovernment Organization
OECD	—	Organisation for Economic Co-operation and Development
PNG	—	Papua New Guinea
PPP	—	Purchasing Power Parity
PRC	—	People's Republic of China
UNESCO	—	United Nations Educational, Scientific and Cultural Organization
UNICEF	—	United Nations Children's Fund

Currency Equivalents
(as of 15 March 2000)

Currency Unit

Peso (P)	P1.00 = $0.02448	$1.00 = P40.8500
Kina (K)	K1.00 = $0.3570	$1.00 = K2.8011

Note

In this booklet, "$" refers to US dollars, unless otherwise specified.

Foreword

The Asian Development Bank (ADB) is a major source of funds and technical advice for the education sector in the Asian and Pacific region. ADB has provided nearly $3.5 billion for education since 1990, representing an average of about 6 percent of total ADB lending per year during that period. ADB recognizes that human development is the basis for national and economic development, and that education – particularly basic education – is a fundamental element of human development. ADB seeks to ensure that its education investment is effectively targeted and efficiently utilized. It further recognizes that a clear policy framework based on careful analysis of the status and development needs of the education sector is necessary for effective investment.

ADB has therefore committed itself to a comprehensive process of review and analysis as the basis for preparing a new education sector policy paper. The policy paper will guide ADB in its support for education in the first years of the 21st century. It will be based on a series of activities, all designed to ensure that the education policy adequately reflects the rapidly evolving circumstances of the region.

ADB commissioned eight country case studies and five technical working papers as inputs to the policy formulation process. The case studies, undertaken by leading education research institutes in the countries concerned, analyzed the issues in education and the policies that had been developed to address the issues. The technical working papers examined selected cross-cutting issues in education development in the region. The case studies and the technical working papers were discussed at a major regional seminar involving representatives of government ministries of education, finance, and planning. Later, the case studies and working papers were integrated into a single publication *Education and National Development in Asia: Trends, Issues, Policies, and Strategies.* This study in turn was an input into ADB's education sector policy paper.

The five technical working papers contain a great deal of useful data and analysis, and it is important to ensure that they are fully available to education policymakers, practitioners, and scholars in the region and elsewhere. Consequently, revised versions are being published separately in their entirety jointly by ADB and the Comparative Education Research Centre of the University of Hong Kong as part of this series entitled *Education in Developing Asia.* ADB hopes that the papers and their wider availability will contribute to a better understanding of the emerging challenges of education development in the region. ADB is pleased to have the partnership of a well-known academic institution in this publication, and thanks the authors and their associates for their contribution.

Nihal Amerasinghe
Director
Agriculture and Social Sectors
Department (East)
Asian Development Bank

Akira Seki
Director
Agriculture and Social Sectors
Department (West)
Asian Development Bank

Introduction

The social and economic development of nations is fundamentally an education process in which people learn to create new institutions, utilize new technologies, cope with their environment, and alter their patterns of behavior. Education in a broad sense improves the capabilities of individuals and the capacity of institutions, and becomes a catalyst for the closely interrelated economic, social, cultural, and demographic changes that become defined as national development. Precisely how these changes occur is not fully known, and this problem often frustrates attempts at national policy making and planning. However, the evidence is substantial that schooling and other forms of education can, in a supporting environment, make major contributions to the complex processes of technology transfer, economic productivity, individual earnings, reduction of poverty, development of healthy families, creation and sharing of values, learning the responsibilities of citizenship, and enhancement of the quality of life.

Yet researchers and scholars also find that education can have negative effects. When formal education is unevenly distributed and is based on inequitable selection practices, it may perpetuate and legitimize social and wealth divisions in society. Further, formal schooling, along with modern media and aspects of global culture, appears to draw children and youth away from their cultural origins and traditional familial customs. Parents from some communities, when faced with school fees and school-leaver unemployment, withdraw their children from school to help them seek alternative paths to their future.

This booklet focuses on the broad role of education in national development in Asia. It emphasizes trends, issues, and envisaged problems within education systems and in the relations between education and the environment. The foremost concerns are the implications for policy making and planning.

The booklet has five main sections:

- First, it describes demographic, economic, social, and education patterns. Descriptions are offered by region, individual countries, and groups of countries.
- Second, it examines relationships between education, economic growth, poverty, and social change. This section includes a review of the education characteristics of a set of countries with highly successful economies. It also looks inside the processes of schooling to discern the effectiveness of instruction and the impediments to learning in the developing member countries (DMCs) of the Asian

1

Development Bank (ADB), and analyzes policy issues by level of education.

- Third, it examines changing patterns of control and responsibility for education decisions. This section provides two national case studies of the decentralization of education governance in DMCs, identifies the possible risks and problems associated with these changes, and analyzes conditions for sustaining new approaches to policy, planning, and practice.

- Fourth, it summarizes trends in major policy areas. This section particularly focuses on governance and management, and highlights ways to provide high-quality education at basic, secondary, and tertiary levels. This section also stresses the need for improved data on education systems.

- Finally, it focuses on ways to develop more effective international assistance. Particular attention is given in this section to the role of ADB.

The Regional Context

Table 1 identifies variations of human development within the Asian and Pacific region. The region has been shaped by many distinctive indigenous cultures, colonization by Western and Asian powers, and the influence of major regional nations, such as the People's Republic of China (PRC) and Japan. East Asia and South Asia have distinctive subregional characteristics. In East Asia, average life expectancies, gross domestic product (GDP) per capita, and literacy rates considerably exceed world averages. South Asia, by contrast, compares unfavorably with other Asian subregions on all development indicators, and has the lowest GDP per capita and literacy rates among the world's regions. Demographic, economic, and social changes within Asia in some cases perpetuate intraregional diversity but in other cases contribute to commonality of issues and policies. These changes and their effects, as described below, can be found in patterns of economic growth, demographic structures, social institutions, and education development.

Demographic Changes

As shown in Table 2, populations of DMCs range from a few thousand in some of the Pacific DMCs to 1.2 billion in the PRC. Annual population growth rates range from -0.2 percent to 3.8 percent. Proportions of population living in urban areas range from 11 percent in Nepal to 100 percent in Singapore. As would be expected, broad differences in life expectancy rates, fertility rates, and infant mortality rates are also found. Fertility rates (measured in live births per woman) range from 1.2 in Hong Kong, China to nearly 7.2 in Marshall Islands, 6.9 in Afghanistan, and 6.7 in Maldives. Hong Kong, China has the longest life expectancy (males 76 years; females 81 years), while Afghanistan has the shortest life expectancy (males 43 years; females 45 years). Hidden in these country averages are wide variations within countries on all of these measures.

Table 1: Regional Comparisons of Human Development, 1997

Region	Life expectancy at birth (Years)		Total fertility rate[a]	GDP per capita (in 1987 US$)	Adult literacy rate (%)	
	Male	Female			Male	Female
East Asia except PRC	69.5	76.2	1.7	7,018	98.2	94.0
South Asia	62.3	63.1	3.3	432	65.0	38.6
SE Asia and the Pacific	63.9	67.9	2.7	1,183	92.2	84.4
All developing countries	63.0	66.1	3.0	908	80.0	62.9
World	64.7	68.9	2.7	3,610	84.3	71.1

[a] Live births per woman

Source: UNDP 1999.

Education and National Development

Table 2: Selected Demographic Conditions

Economy	Population Total 1997 (millions)	Average annual growth rate 1990-1997 (%)	Urban population 1997 (% of total)	Dependency[a] ratio of 0-14 1995 (% of total population)
Afghanistan	18	2.0[b]	20[c]	40.8
Bangladesh	124	1.6	19	39.5
Bhutan	—	—	—	41.1
Cambodia	11	2.7	22	44.9
PRC	1,227	1.2	30[c]	26.4
Cook Islands	0.02	1.9	60[c]	34.1
Fiji Islands	0.8	1.6	41[c]	34.7
Hong Kong, China	7	1.9	95	19.2
India	961	1.9	27[c]	35.2
Indonesia	200	1.7	37	33.0
Kazakhstan	16	(0.2)	60[c]	29.8
Kiribati	0.08	2.3	36[c]	40.3
Korea, Republic of	46	1.0	83	23.6
Kyrgyz Republic	5	0.7	39	37.1
Lao PDR	3	2.6	22	44.8
Malaysia	21	2.3	55	38.0
Maldives	262	3.5	27[c]	46.6
Marshall Islands	0.06	3.8	69[c]	50.6
Micronesia, F.S.	0.1	1.1	28[c]	—
Mongolia	3	2.1	62	38.0
Myanmar	45	1.9	26[c]	37.4
Nauru	—	1.9[d]	14[c]	—
Nepal	23	2.7	11	42.4
Pakistan	137	2.9	35	44.3
Papua New Guinea	5	2.3	17	39.5
Philippines	73	2.3	56	38.3
Samoa	0.1	0.4	21[c]	46.3
Singapore	3	1.9	100	22.7
Solomon Islands	0.4	3.7	17[c]	44.2
Sri Lanka	18	1.2	23	30.6
Taipei,China	21	1.0	57[c]	24.1
Thailand	61	1.2	21	28.3
Tonga	0.1	0.3	41[c]	—
Tuvalu	0.01	1.4	46[c]	—
Uzbekistan	—	2.2[d]	41[c]	43.4
Vanuatu	0.2	2.7	19[c]	39.9
Viet Nam	77	2.1	20	37.4

— Data not available.

Notes: (1) Data in parentheses are negative.

(2) Data in italics are for years or periods other than those specified in the column heading.

[a] Estimated data using medium variant projections except for Cook Islands, Kiribati, and Marshall Islands.

Life expectancy at birth 1996 (years)		Total fertility rate 1996 (per woman)	Infant mortality rate 1996 (per 1,000 live births)	Economy
Male	*Female*			
43	45	6.9	—	Afghanistan
57	59	3.4	77	Bangladesh
—	—	5.9	—	Bhutan
52	55	4.6	105	Cambodia
68	71	1.9	33	PRC
—	—	—	—	Cook Islands
70	74	2.8	22	Fiji Islands
76	81	1.2	4	Hong Kong, China
61	61	3.2	68	India
63	67	2.6	49	Indonesia
65	74	2.3	62	Kazakhstan
56	58	3.8	65	Kiribati
69	76	1.7	9	Korea, Republic of
62	71	3.0	26	Kyrgyz Republic
52	54	5.7	101	Lao PDR
70	74	3.4	11	Malaysia
63	61	6.7	55	Maldives
61	64	7.2	55	Marshall Islands
—	—	5.1	37	Micronesia, F.S.
64	67	3.3	53	Mongolia
57	60	4.1	82	Myanmar
—	—	—	—	Nauru
57	57	5.0	85	Nepal
62	65	5.1	88	Pakistan
57	58	4.7	62	Papua New Guinea
64	68	3.6	37	Philippines
67	71	4.3	23	Samoa
74	79	1.7	4	Singapore
61	63	5.2	42	Solomon Islands
71	75	2.3	15	Sri Lanka
72	78	1.8	5	Taipei,China
67	72	1.8	34	Thailand
67	71	3.4	19	Tonga
—	—	—	38	Tuvalu
66	72	3.7	30	Uzbekistan
59	61	5.1	47	Vanuatu
66	70	3.0	40	Viet Nam

[b] Figures may be influenced by refugees to an unknown extent.
[c] Based on national definitions incorporated in the latest available census.
[d] Annual population growth rates refer to the growth of the population for the last five years available.

Source: World Bank 1998.

The demographic change taking place in Asia is basically a transition from high mortality and fertility to lower mortality and fertility. Mortality and fertility declines have followed a pattern of demographic divergence, with Northeast Asia entering demographic transition early, and South Asia later. Variations in demographic structures help explain economic growth rates, and have given East Asia an advantage over South Asia. During the next few decades, the demographic factors that contributed to success in East Asia are likely to work to South Asia's relative advantage (ADB 1997). The impact on the age structure of Asia's population and on all social and economic sectors will continue to be enormous. Over the last three decades demographic change has contributed to economic growth and indirectly to education growth, particularly for males, by increasing the growth rate of the economically active population. This condition was most observable in East Asia. However, income growth has been retarded in countries with large youth or dependency ratios and thus with implied high-consumption needs.

The quantity and quality of schooling are influenced by demographic structures, and are sensitive to the size of school-age cohorts. Thus, richer DMCs with lower dependency ratios have been able to invest more per child with similar allocations of funds. High dependency ratios in poorer countries, by forcing choices as to which children go to school, tend to be associated with suppression of female enrollments and thus indirectly may reduce the number of opportunities in the labor market for females (Lewin 1996, 50). The projected decline in Asian dependency rates may make more resources available and provide an opportunity to concentrate on improvements in the quality of education.

The urban-rural mix of population is also changing rapidly in several DMCs. Generally, Asia is becoming increasingly urbanized, accompanying the decline in the size of the agriculture sector and the increase in industrialization. Continued urbanization can be expected in the 21st century. For example, in Indonesia 31 percent of the population in 1990 lived in urban areas. However, by 2005, it is estimated that over half of the Indonesian population will be urban dwellers. DMCs that have higher urban population ratios tend to have lower dependency ratios, longer life expectancies, lower mortality and fertility rates, and better Human Development Index (HDI), Human Poverty Index (HPI), and Gender-related Development Index (GDI) rankings. The more urban DMCs also have higher per capita incomes and higher percentages of their labor forces in industry and services. Urbanization brings new opportunities and new problems to education. Higher enrollments may be expected, and also better facilities in the urban areas. However, addressing the education needs of the growing numbers of marginalized urban poor will demand special resources and programs.

Economic Changes

Economic indicators demonstrate a broad range of rates of economic growth, incidence of poverty, and patterns of employment by sector among DMCs. The regional average GDP per capita, in purchasing power parity (PPP) dollars in 1993, was approximately $4,600. As shown in Table 3, GDP per capita among DMCs in 1997 ranged from $200 to $22,500. Other data show that the average regional economic growth rate between 1985 and 1995 was approximately 7 percent. This record has transformed many DMCs, and made Asia economically the fastest-growing continent. However, a fiscal crisis and economic downturn in East and Southeast Asia which began in 1998 significantly dampened economic growth.

Demand for schooling reflects changes in employment patterns (Table 3). In the high-performing, newly industrialized economies (NIEs) – Hong Kong,

Table 3: Economic and Social Conditions

Economy	GDP per capita Year 1997 ($)	Average annual growth 1996-97 (%)	Labor Force Agriculture 1997 (%)	Labor Force Industry 1997 (%)	Labor Force Services 1997 (%)	GDP share of agriculture 1994 (%)	Adult illiteracy 1995 (%)	Population in poverty <$1(PPP) a day 1989-1994 (%)	HDI Rank 1997
Afghanistan	—	—	—	—	—	—	68.5	—	—
Bangladesh	220	2.1	24	27	49	30	61.9	—	144
Bhutan	400	2.8	38	38	25	—	57.8	—	155
Cambodia	—	—	51	15	34	—	—	—	153
PRC	530	8.3	19	49	32	21	18.5	29.4	108
Fiji Islands	2,470	(0.5)	18	26	56	—	8.4	—	46
Hong Kong, China	21,650	4.8	1	15	84	0	7.8	—	22
India	320	3.2	25	30	45	30	48	52.5	138
Indonesia	880	6.0	16	43	41	17	16.2	14.5	99
Kazakhstan	1,160	(8.6)	12	27	61	44	—	—	93
Kiribati	910	(0.5)	—	—	—	—	—	—	—
Korea, Republic of	8,620	7.7	6	43	51	7	2.0	—	32
Kyrgyz Republic	630	(6.9)	45	23	33	37	—	18.9	107
Lao PDR	320	2.7	52	21	26	51	43.4	—	136
Malaysia	3,480	5.7	12	47	41	14	16.5	5.6	60
Maldives	1,150	3.3	32	31	37	—	6.8	—	111
Marshall Islands	1,770	—	—	—	—	—	—	—	—
Micronesia, F.S.	1,980	—	—	—	—	—	—	—	—
Mongolia	300	(3.8)	37	23	40	21	—	—	101
Myanmar	—	—	59	10	31	63	16.9	—	131
Nepal	200	2.4	41	22	36	44	72.5	53.1	154
Pakistan	430	1.2	25	25	50	25	62.2	11.6	139
Papua New Guinea	1,240	2.3	28	36	36	28	27.8	—	128
Philippines	950	1.5	19	32	49	22	5.4	27.5	98
Singapore	22,500	6.2	0	35	65	0	8.9	—	26
Solomon Islands	900	(1.5)	—	—	—	—	—	—	122
Sri Lanka	640	2.6	22	26	52	24	9.8	4.0	91
Thailand	2,410	8.4	11	40	49	10	6.2	0.1	59
Tonga	1,830	(0.4)	—	—	—	—	—	—	—
Uzbekistan	—	(3.9)	32	27	41	33	0.3	—	100
Vanuatu	—	—	25	12	63	—	—	—	124
Viet Nam	200	—	26	31	43	28	6.3	—	121

— Data not available.

Notes: (1) Data in parentheses are negative.
        (2) Data in italics are for years or periods other than those specified in the column heading.

Sources: UNDP 1990, 1999; UNESCO, Division of Statistics 1999; World Bank 1996, 1998.

China; Republic of Korea; Singapore; and Taipei,China – industries and services together account for over 90 percent of the labor force. Increasingly, the service sectors of those economies, which dominate employment with over 50 percent of the labor force, require high information technologies, interpersonal skills, and analytical capabilities. In other country groupings the mix is quite different. Trends in the female share of the labor force are difficult to determine. Highly agricultural countries, which utilize low levels of technology, commonly employ large percentages of women. Likewise, countries with export-oriented industries may employ many women in entry-level jobs.

Data by country on any of the poverty indices are limited. From data available, the range of percentage of population in poverty (<PPP$1 a day) varies from 0.1 percent in Thailand to 53.1 percent in Nepal. The NIEs – also known as the "four tigers" – have relatively small incidences of poverty. Higher percentages of population in poverty tend to be found in countries with high percentages of the labor force in agriculture. HDI, HPI, and GDI country rankings are correlated with each other, and the higher the rankings of countries on these indices, the lower their population growth rates, illiteracy rates, and GDP shares in agriculture.

The most impressive economic gains have been in East Asia, particularly in the NIEs, which between 1985 and 1995 averaged 6.2 percent annual growth. Other rapidly growing economies include the PRC, Malaysia, and Thailand, which (starting at lower economic levels than the NIEs) averaged 7.5 percent annual economic growth per capita between 1985 and 1995. During the same decade, significant economic advances were made by several other DMCs, including Indonesia and the Philippines. East Asia's pattern of economic growth was characterized by:

- early development of a broad base of human capital through a focus on basic education;
- an outward-looking trade strategy;
- relatively equitable distribution of benefits of economic growth;
- reforms to encourage savings; and
- a cooperative relationship between public and private sectors.

Other countries, particularly those in South Asia, have not fared so well (Table 4). Haq (1997) described South Asia as "the poorest region; the most illiterate; the most malnourished region; the least gender sensitive region; the region with highest human deprivation; and the most militarized region in the world." South Asia, Haq concluded, followed inefficient, centralized, economic planning; had closed international markets which emphasized domestic protection; and invested relatively little in education. For example, Haq recorded, the amount invested per pupil rose by 355 percent in the Republic of Korea between 1970 and 1990, but only by 13 percent in Pakistan.

Economic growth has contributed much to national development. Growth has been associated with expansion of opportunities in education, availability of health services, and improved quality of life. Economic growth has provided employment opportunities for women, and consequently helped support

Table 4a: NIEs and South Asia Comparison

Region	GDP per capita		Share of GDP in agriculture 1994 (%)	Adult illiteracy rate 1995 (%)	Dependency ratio 1997 (%)
	1994 ($)	Growth rate 1985-95 (%)			
NIEs	17,590	6.2	7.0	6.2	21.3
South Asia	372.5	2.1	30.8	55.5	39.3

Table 4b: NIEs and South Asia Comparison
(percent)

Region	First-level education			Second-level education GER 1993	Third-level education GER 1993
	GER 1993	P/T ratio 1993	Repeaters 1993		
NIEs	97.0	26.5	1.0	92.0	37.6
South Asia	82.8	40.2	11.7	44.3	5.5

GER = Gross Enrollment Rate; P/T = Pupil/Teacher.

Sources: UNESCO 1996; UNESCO, Division of Statistics 1999; World Bank 1997.

their families. Income has in many cases added to the independence of women. However, there have been negative as well as positive consequences of economic growth. For example, much of the work in the export industries has placed women in unhealthy conditions and increased their susceptibility to certain diseases. Moreover, these industries have offered few transferable skills to allow employment in other industries.

Economic growth is generally associated with higher enrollments: an important but insufficient condition for quality education. Slower-growth countries tend to have high rates of truancy, more heavily utilize child labor, and are plagued with high repetition and dropout rates. Economic growth does not always translate into education improvements, however: per capita incomes in Pakistan and Papua New Guinea (PNG) are high compared with social sector development. Nor is a low incidence of poverty necessarily directly linked to education achievement. For example, Kerala and Rajasthan are two of India's rural states which have similar levels of poverty; but female literacy varies from 85 percent in the former to 12 percent in the latter.

Social Changes

Changes and continued diversity may be found in all social institutions. At the family level, the last few decades have seen significant changes in family size, familial roles, and intergenerational relations. The average size of families is declining in several DMCs, in some countries radically so. Smaller families and higher education and economic levels of parents, especially of mothers, tend to alter the treatment of children in the home, improve children's health, and increase children's education opportunities. However, a growing education gap between the generations and the economic mobility of younger employees – a characteristic of modern production – places stress on family relationships.

Transition from an extended to nuclear family structure is likely to continue, further altering familial relations and obligations. Reflecting the extent of social and familial change, divorce rates have risen, and new laws in Singapore and Taipei,China require children to be responsible for the welfare of their aging parents.

The rapidity of technological change as reflected in new forms of production and global communication compresses the available time for individual and social adaptation. Typically, the young, better educated, and urban populations more readily understand, accept, or learn to cope with emerging new values, attitudes, and lifestyles. At times, opportunities for added income from new industries for females has directly altered family structures. Some evidence is reported in Thailand for example, where the preference for sons is said to be disappearing. On the other hand, there are cases where the incomes from young women wage earners have been utilized by the family primarily to increase advancement opportunities for the sons.

Changes in that most macro of institutions, the state, are also evolving significantly. Many forms of government and differing roles of the state's involvement in the economic and education sectors can be found in Asia. An orientation toward capitalism and private markets has a long history in some economies, such as Hong Kong, China and the Republic of Korea. Although socialist states such as the PRC, the Lao People's Democratic Republic (Lao PDR), and Viet Nam are now more responsive to privatization, this trend cuts across economic and political differences. In the education sector this movement is particularly visible in higher education, but is growing also at the primary and secondary school levels. Even in countries where constitutional provisions guarantee free education (e.g., Cambodia, Mongolia, and Philippines), user charges are necessary to support schools even in the public sector (Bray 1996).

Paralleling or encompassing enlargement of the private sector, the locus of public decision making – traditionally centralized – is under modification or review. A distinct regional trend has been evident, albeit more pervasive in some countries than in others. PRC, India, and Thailand are among countries with far-reaching devolution of social services and institutions. Most DMCs are committed in varying degrees to the strengthening of local government and to a degree of decentralization in the delivery of education. As this trend evolves, the focal point for some social and education policy making and much planning will transfer from the center to provincial and lower levels of government.

Cultural and social changes have meant that the roles and opportunities for many Asian women have altered and will continue to evolve. Major inequities remain, but increased opportunities for work, smaller families, more schooling, and new values and role models have combined to raise consciousness about gender disparities. International organizations, nongovernment organizations (NGOs), and many governments have increased their attention to the specific problems associated with efforts to secure equitable gender treatment in the home, school, and workplace. Improvements can be demonstrated, particularly in increased opportunities in education and improved health. Yet, in 1990 less than 8 percent of the women aged 18-22 were enrolled in education institutions compared with over 11 percent for men in the same age cohort. Moreover, only 10 percent of the formal labor market in Asia were women. The main avenue of employment for women remains traditional agriculture.

Many of these demographic, economic, and social changes, including education growth, reflect the strength of national social and political commitments to improve the welfare of citizens. Generally, living standards have been on the rise in DMCs. There is a tendency for people to live longer, be more literate, eat better, and go to school for longer periods.

Along with improvements in the quality of life for many, poverty exists on a huge scale. One third of the total population of the world lives in poverty, and three quarters of the world's impoverished live in Asia. There is, for example, a 36-year difference in female life expectancy within the region. Large disparities in access to health, education, and social services exist between countries, between areas within countries, between rural and urban populations, between ethnic groups, and between the sexes.

Economic growth and social changes have not always proportionately lowered the incidence of poverty or improved the quality of life for all. Exceptions include Sri Lanka, where the incomes of the poor grew faster, and Thailand, where, despite economic growth, the incomes of the poor lagged. World Bank and ADB documents conclude that poverty is reduced most successfully through the initiation of policies along the lines of those demonstrated in East Asia. Growth strategies to yield the largest poverty-reduction benefits appear to include:

- rapid growth of labor-intensive production across a wide front, led by exports;
- expansion of poor people's access to physical and financial capital via labor-intensive manufacturing exports and agricultural productivity which promote rural development;
- mass basic education to ease the transition from the agricultural to the industrial economy; and
- an increase of human capital via targeting of the expansion of primary, nonformal, and literacy education, especially in rural and poor urban areas.

Education Development

The meanings and purposes of education and the patterns of development of education systems have been profoundly influenced by history and by recent economic and cultural changes in the region. Mass education systems utilizing local languages are a relatively recent phenomenon in many DMCs. Even more recent are the views of education as a basic human need, an integral part of quality of life, a support for moral and social values, and an instrument for economic productivity.

Education and National Development

Table 5: Gross Enrollment Rates by Education Level, 1975-2010 (percent)

Economy	First-level education					Second-level education					Third-level education				
	1975	1985	1993[a]	2000[b]	2010[b]	1975	1985	1993[a]	2000[b]	2010[b]	1975	1985	1993[a]	2000[b]	2010[b]
Afghanistan	25	20	48	27	23	—	—	22	11	11	1	—	—	2	2
Bangladesh	73	64	—	80	82	19	18	—	22	23	—	5	—	4	4
Bhutan	9	27	—	36	39	1	—	—	8	9	—	—	—	0.3	0.4
Cambodia	—	—	118	—	—	—	—	25	—	—	—	—	1	—	—
PRC	122	123	118	120	114	46	39	55	55	66	1	3	4	3	3
Fiji Islands	137	122	128	122	119	44	51	64	71	78	3	3	—	15	16
Hong Kong, China	119	105	99	108	108	49	71	85	84	87	10	13	23	26	33
India	81	96	102	106	109	28	37	49	50	54	9	6	—	10	11
Indonesia	86	117	115	115	111	20	41	45	63	70	2	—	9	11	13
Kazakhstan	—	88	87	—	—	—	103	91	—	—	—	37	34	—	—
Korea, Rep. of	107	97	95	107	107	56	92	99	101	102	10	34	55	46	51
Kyrgyz Republic	—	123	111	—	—	—	110	86	—	—	—	28	20	—	—
Lao PDR	67	111	107	116	121	8	23	25	27	30	37	2	2	1	2
Malaysia	94	101	93	95	95	46	53	61	62	67	—	6	10	14	18
Maldives	—	—	134	148	149	—	—	49	34	34	—	—	—	—	—
Mongolia	108	101	84	97	94	81	92	60	95	101	8	22	14	20	21
Myanmar	83	98	100	125	125	—	23	30	36	40	—	5	5	8	9
Nepal	51	75	109	91	91	13	25	36	32	33	2	4	5	6	6
Pakistan	41	44	69	46	49	15	17	—	20	21	2	3	—	3	3
PNG	57	—	82	78	81	12	—	14	16	19	3	2	3	4	5
Philippines	107	107	111	108	106	54	64	80	81	84	18	25	27	34	36
Singapore	110	115	—	107	106	52	62	—	75	77	9	14	35	33	34
Solomon Islands	—	79	97	—	—	—	19	17	—	—	—	—	—	—	—
Sri Lanka	77	103	105	108	109	48	63	75	76	76	1	4	6	7	8
Thailand	84	96	87	90	89	25	30	49	38	45	4	19	21	20	24
Uzbekistan	—	87	77	—	—	—	107	93	—	—	—	30	32	—	—
Vanuatu	—	100	106	—	—	—	—	—	—	—	—	—	—	—	—
Viet Nam	107	103	114	106	105	39	43	41	49	52	2	2	3	2	2

— Data not available.
[a] Data are by approximation.
[b] Data for 2000 and 2010 are projections by UNESCO.

Sources: UNESCO 1989, 1993, 1996.

Table 5 shows that primary education has approached universalization in many economies. The mean gross enrollment rate (GER) for first-level education for DMCs was 100 percent in 1993 as compared with 83 percent in 1975. However, even with significant overall enrollment growth, a large percentage of girls in the age cohort remain out of school. Further, the female share of the population of teachers remained much the same between 1980 and 1995. Costly inefficiencies in primary schooling remain, as reflected in the large numbers of overage children, repeaters, and dropouts.

The development of second-level education shows large intraregional differences. In Afghanistan only 11 percent of girls are enrolled at this level as compared with 99 percent in the Republic of Korea. Kazakhstan, Kyrgyz Republic, and to a lesser extent, Philippines, Thailand, and Uzbekistan, are positive outliers. The trends from 1975 to 1993 generally show enrollment growth, with some areas showing considerable growth. Indonesia, for example, had over 100 percent growth. However, as shown in Table 5, the late 1980s brought a decrease in secondary enrollments, which has not yet been fully explained. In several economies, presumably some combination of wage-earning opportunities, poor quality and relevance of schooling, and the level of school fees and other costs reduced demand. Data in Table 5 for 2000 and 2010 are United Nations Educational, Scientific and Cultural Organization (UNESCO) projections, which do not always appear compatible with the data shown earlier. The projections anticipate continued upward growth patterns with some increases in efficiency in first-level education.

Generally, the pattern of education expansion follows the pattern of economic growth, with high levels of economic growth associated with high education enrollments. A sharp economic downturn in the 1990s negatively affected some countries that had a tradition of high literacy and levels of school enrollment, e.g., Kazakhstan, Kyrgyz Republic, and Uzbekistan. Yet, at any given economic level there is a wide variation in education development.

As described in the Figure and Table 6, total regional education expenditure as a percentage of GDP and as a percentage of government expenditure shows different patterns of change across the period 1975-1994.

The percentages of GDP spent on education appear to have stabilized. However, as shown in Table 6, there is room for considerable increase in countries such as Indonesia and the Philippines.

Figure: Total Regional Public Education Expenditure

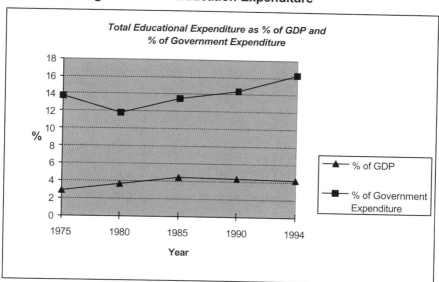

Sources: UNESCO 1989, 1996.

Education and National Development

Table 6: Total Regional Public Education Expenditure
(percent)

Economy	Percentage of GDP					Percentage of government expenditure				
	1975	1980	1985	1990	1995/96	1975	1980	1985	1990	1995/96
Afghanistan	1.5	2.0	—	—	—	—	12.7	—	—	—
Bangladesh	1.4	1.5	1.9	2.0	2.9	13.6	7.8	9.7	10.3	8.7
Bhutan	—	—	3.7	—	—	—	—	—	—	—
Cambodia	—	—	—	—	2.9	—	—	—	—	1.8
PRC	—	2.5	2.6	2.3	2.3	—	9.3	12.2	12.8	11.9
Cook Islands	—	—	—	—	—	—	—	9.5	—	12.4
Fiji Islands	4.7	5.9	6.0	4.7	5.4	19.5	11.3	—	—	18.6
Hong Kong, China	3.0	—	—	—	2.8	20.7	14.6	18.4	17.4	17.0
India	2.9	2.8	3.4	3.9	3.5	9.4	10.0	9.4	10.9	11.6
Indonesia	2.7	1.7	—	1.1	1.4	13.1	—	—	—	7.9
Kazakhstan	—	—	6.5	6.5	4.7	—	—	18.9	17.6	17.6
Kiribati	4.9	—	6.7	6.0	6.3	—	—	18.5	18.3	17.6
Korea, Republic of	2.2	3.7	4.5	3.5	3.7	13.9	—	—	—	17.4
Kyrgyz Republic	—	7.2	7.9	8.5	5.7	—	22.2	22.4	22.5	23.5
Lao PDR	—	—	—	2.3	2.5	—	—	—	—	—
Malaysia	6.0	6.0	6.6	5.4	5.2	19.3	14.7	16.3	18.3	15.5
Maldives	—	4.4	6.3	11.6	6.4	—	—	7.2	10.0	10.5
Mongolia	—	7.8	8.6	8.5	6.4	—	—	—	17.6	19.3
Myanmar	1.7	1.7	2.0	2.4	1.2	15.3	—	—	—	14.4
Nepal	1.5	1.8	2.6	2.0	3.1	11.5	10.5	12.7	8.5	13.5
Pakistan	2.2	2.0	2.5	2.6	3.0	5.2	5.0	—	—	8.1
Papua New Guinea	—	4.7	—	—	—	—	14.2	—	—	—
Philippines	1.9	1.7	1.4	2.9	2.2	11.4	9.1	7.4	10.1	—
Singapore	2.9	2.8	4.4	3.1	3.0	8.6	7.3	—	18.2	23.4
Solomon Islands	—	5.6	4.7	4.2	—	14.7	11.2	12.4	7.9	—
Sri Lanka	2.8	2.7	2.6	2.7	3.4	10.1	7.7	6.9	8.1	8.9
Taipei,China	—	—	—	—	—	—	—	—	—	—
Thailand	3.5	3.4	3.8	3.6	4.1	21.0	20.6	18.5	20.0	20.1
Tonga	3.0	—	4.4	4.8	4.7	12.7	11.6	16.1	17.3	17.3
Tuvalu	—	—	—	—	—	—	—	—	16.2	—
Uzbekistan	—	—	—	9.5	8.1	—	—	—	—	21.1
Vanuatu	—	—	—	4.4	4.9	—	—	—	—	—
Viet Nam	—	—	—	—	2.7	—	—	—	—	7.4

— Data not available.

Sources: UNESCO 1989, 1998.

The growth of percentage of government expenditures could climb somewhat higher, although most governments are reluctant to spend more than 20 percent of their budgets on education. Like all education indicators, those on expenditures at best tell an incomplete story. Many types of financial support for schools and other education programs are not calculated within the typically reported expenditures. Even more subtly, there is room to maneuver within the same amount of available fiscal resources. That is, talented administrators, imaginative teachers, and enthusiastic parents can obtain additional returns on given levels of resources (Bray 2002).

A caveat is necessary in discussing education development: the accuracy of the available data is questionable. Levels of enrollment, literacy rates, and expenditures are often subject to debate. Box 1 provides an example of the uncertainty of education statistics in Nepal. The situation described is not uncommon among DMCs.

The organization of education systems and curricula vary somewhat by country. The first level of education tends to be organized into one level of primary education of four to eight years, but most typically has to five or six years. The general secondary level is commonly divided into two levels, the first of which increasingly has been associated with primary education to form formal basic education. Higher education varies widely in length depending on the course of study.

Preprimary enrollments are increasing, but still typically represent a small fraction of the age cohort. In all likelihood, given its importance, the preprimary level, although highly influenced by economic conditions, will increase in the coming decades. Basic education, which in the 1990s emerged as the highest priority, is increasingly extended to include junior secondary education. A common core curriculum of mathematics, science, and language is usually found in each country. National variations tend to be found in language of instruction, and local options, such as local language and customs, are commonly allowed within national policy.

Many systems have inequitable characteristics in the nature of expansion and development of their education systems. Particularly above the primary level, the poorest segments of the population are rarely accommodated until most middle- and upper-income groups are well represented. However, the meaning of education opportunity may not be the same for those who enter last as for those who enter early. As the system fills up, the qualifications required to obtain employment and economic benefits are raised. Thus, without powerful intervention through targeted policies, the poor may be chasing a moving target of potential rewards.

A Typology of Developing Member Countries

For convenience in intraregional analysis, DMCs are grouped into seven categories, a loose classification system used in prior ADB documents.[1] The Lewin (1996) grouping is partly defined by sets of indicators that include demographic factors, economic factors, employment factors, levels of literacy, and Human Development Index (HDI). This classification does not constitute a formal typology developed from a rigid set of common criteria, but is a device for facilitating comparisons of education development and for capturing the variations in education's external linkages with other sectors. Other groupings of DMCs will be explored as important comparisons across DMCs are examined. Moreover, even though sets of DMCs group together fairly well on certain economic and social indicators, this does not necessarily mean that similar policies need to be developed. Variations in cultural and social values

---

[1] See the six groups found in *Education and Development* (ADB 1991); and the seven groups found in *Access to Education in Emerging Asia* (Lewin 1996).

Box 1: Case of Inconsistent Data – Nepal

In Nepal, the gross and net enrollment rates for 1995 that were made official by the Ministry of Education and those published by the Central Bureau of Statistics, National Planning Commission, were substantially different. Neither the Ministry of Education nor the National Planning Commission made any clarification regarding such a huge discrepancy between the two sets of the same indicators. The Ministry of Education data were based on the information that the Ministry had received from schools, while the National Planning Commission data were based on a national sample survey of 3,388 households.

So far, the Ministry data have been used both nationally and internationally. But new rates that the National Planning Commission disclosed raised questions about the Ministry statistics. In any case, basic indicators such as the net and gross enrollment rates are important, and it is urgently necessary that the Government fulfill its responsibility by making public the accurate national statistics, with scientific explanations. The process of planning education resources and activities relies heavily on these indicators.

Source: Shakya et al. 1998.

and political conditions may result in a wide array of policies and programs (see Tables 7, 8, and 9).

Group 1 consists of the PRC and India, which contain over 60 percent of the population of all DMCs. The GDP per capita for these two DMCs is between \$320 and \$530. These DMCs are between 26.8 percent and 30.3 percent urbanized, and the majority of their labor forces remain in agriculture. They share low HDI rankings: 108 for the PRC and 135 for India. The economic growth rate for the PRC is much higher than that for India, while the population growth rate is much lower.

Table 7: DMC Groupings

Group 1	Group 2	Group 3	Group 4	Group 5	Group 6	Group 7
PRC	Hong Kong,	Indonesia	Bangladesh	Afghanistan	Kazakhstan	Cook Islands
India	China	Pakistan	Mongolia	Bhutan	Kyrgyz	Fiji Islands
	Republic of	Philippines	Myanmar	Cambodia	Republic	Kiribati
	Korea	Sri Lanka	Viet Nam	Lao PDR	Uzbekistan	Maldives
	Malaysia	Thailand		Nepal		Marshall Islands
	Singapore					Micronesia, F.S.
	Taipei,China					Nauru
						PNG
						Solomon Islands
						Tonga
						Tuvalu
						Vanuatu
						Samoa

PRC = People's Republic of China
Lao PDR = Lao People's Democratic Republic
PNG = Papua New Guinea

Group 2 includes the NIEs – Hong Kong, China; Republic of Korea; Singapore; and Taipei,China. The average GDP per capita is $14,062, and HDI ranks are between 22 and 60. These economies are highly urbanized, and have had high economic growth rates and high indices of education development. Because of these conditions, Malaysia is sometimes associated with this group.

Group 3 comprises countries that have achieved substantial economic growth but in which GDP per capita remains significantly lower than Group 2. This group includes Indonesia, Philippines, Sri Lanka, and Thailand. Pakistan is sometimes associated with this group. The HDI rankings for this group range between 59 and 139. Agriculture remains a significant employer in these countries. Thailand is the richest and fastest-growing DMC of this group.

Group 4 contains countries with low levels of economic development and generally low levels of economic growth. Countries in this group are Bangladesh, Mongolia, Myanmar, and Viet Nam. HDI ranks for this group range between 101 and 144.

Group 5 comprises low GDP per capita countries that also have low HDI rankings. These countries are predominantly agricultural. The countries include Afghanistan, Bhutan, Cambodia, Lao PDR, and Nepal. The HDI range for these countries is between 136 and 155. On several indicators this is the poorest and least educationally developed of the seven groups.

Group 6 countries, Kazakhstan, Kyrgyz Republic, and Uzbekistan were formerly part of the Soviet Union but became independent states in 1991. These countries have low per capita GDP, with wide variations in degree of industrial development. This group has comparatively high education development, but has experienced declines in secondary and tertiary enrollment and a deteriorating quality of instruction.

Group 7 includes the Pacific DMCs, which have small populations and exhibit extensive variation on economic, social, and education indicators. Included in Group 7 are Cook Islands, Fiji Islands, Kiribati, Maldives, Papua New Guinea, Samoa, Solomon Islands, Tonga, Tuvalu, and Vanuatu. The populations of these countries range from 10,000 (Tuvalu) to nearly 5 million (Papua New Guinea). The HDI ranks fall between 46 (Fiji Islands) and 128 (Papua New Guinea).

Further examination of these country groupings reveals intragroup and cross-group similarities. The NIEs (Group 2) share the following characteristics: large urban population, high life expectancy, low fertility, low mortality, and low dependency ratio. These characteristics and the economic and education policies of Group 2 will be analyzed below. Groups 2 and 6 stand out with high literacy and enrollment rates, reflecting their already well-developed education systems. For example, in these economies, first-level education is essentially universal and second-level gross enrollment rates exceed 80 percent. Moreover, children who enroll in school tend to stay in school (children not reaching Grade 5 in Group 6 is 0 percent; in Group 2, 0.7 percent).

Groups 4 and 5 have high dropout and repetition rates, high illiteracy rates, and low enrollment rates. Of all the groups, Group 5 spends the smallest share of gross national product (GNP) on education, reflecting low economic development. Most of the countries in Groups 4 and 5 have less than 25 percent of the age cohort finishing the basic education cycle on schedule.

Almost everybody in the countries of Group 6 is literate, both males and females, compared with a 40 percent literacy rate in Group 5. Countries with very high illiteracy rates include Nepal (72.5 percent), Afghanistan (68.5 percent), Pakistan (62.2 percent), and Bangladesh (61.9 percent). Countries with lower literacy rates tend to have larger gender gaps, although there are considerable variations within each group.

India, Maldives, and Papua New Guinea have more than 130 percent GERs at the first level of education, which implies that there are many overage children and repeaters in primary school. Bangladesh, Kazakhstan, Malaysia, Singapore, Uzbekistan, and Vanuatu have almost 100 percent intake rates with low percentages of repeaters. Afghanistan has the lowest enrollment rates for all categories: males 41 percent and females 14 percent. Group 5 has a large gender difference in the enrollment of students in the first level, while there are no gender gaps at this level in Groups 2 and 6. Groups 2 and 6 demonstrate high efficiency in the first level of education, with almost all the students reaching Grade 5. Examples are the Republic of Korea, Singapore, Uzbekistan (100 percent), and Malaysia (98 percent). In Group 5, only 60 percent of the students stay in school until Grade 5.

Table 8: Adult Illiteracy Rates, 1995
(percent)

Group	Countries	Mean	Minimum	Maximum
1	2	33.3	18.5	48.0
2	4	8.8	2.0	16.5
3	5	19.9	5.4	62.2
4	3	28.4	6.3	61.9
5	4	60.5	43.4	72.5
6	1	0.3	0.3	0.3
7	3	14.3	6.8	27.8
Total	22	26.0	0.3	72.7

Sources: UNESCO 1989, 1998.

Table 9: Mid-Year Population, 1995
(millions)

Group	Countries	Mean	Minimum	Maximum
1	2	1060.7	916.5	1204.9
2	5	19.1	3.0	44.9
3	5	94.6	18.0	195.3
4	4	59.5	2.3	116.9
5	5	11.0	1.7	20.6
6	2	10.6	4.5	16.6
7	12	0.5	0.01	4.1

Sources: UNESCO 1989, 1998.

In terms of public expenditure on education, Group 7 spends the largest share of GDP (6.9 percent) of all the groups, while Group 5 spends the smallest share (2.9 percent). Countries in Group 6 (Kyrgyz Republic at 6.8 percent) and Group 7 (Maldives 8.1 percent; Kiribati 7.4 percent) gather at the top end of percentage of GDP allocated by the government to education, while the countries in Group 5 (Lao PDR 2.3 percent; Bhutan 2.7 percent; Nepal 2.9 percent) allocate the smallest amounts to education development. The governments of about half of all the countries spend less than 3.8 percent of GDP on education. However, nongovernment expenditures may be substantial in some countries (Bray 1996; Tan and Mingat 1992).

The transition economies of the former Soviet Union (Group 6) share a heritage of pre-transition, public ownership, and a high level of provision of education and other public services relative to their economic development. Two of Group 6, Kazakhstan and the Kyrgyz Republic, can expect a slow growth of the school-age population during the next decade. Nevertheless, maintenance of a high level of public provision of schooling may be difficult.

Groups 2 and 6 reflect a high enrollment of third-level students, averaging about 2,500 per 100,000 inhabitants – more than 1,000 students greater than Group 3's enrollment average, and much higher than Group 5's enrollment figure of 228 per 100,000 population. The wide range in the number of third-level students can be at least partly explained by the range of economic and demographic differences between the countries in the region. Additional explanations center on the variation in political responses to social demand.

Education, Economic Growth,
and Social Change

This section analyzes links between education and economic growth, giving special attention to the economic and education experiences of the NIEs. It also explores linkages between education and poverty. A brief look is taken at core activities in education, teaching, and learning; and trends and strategies are examined for each major education subsector.

Education and Economic Growth

Economic growth is important for national development. Economic growth is generally assumed to be explained largely by stocks of labor, physical capital, and human capital (improvement in the quality of the labor force). Technology is assumed to be part of the growth equation, and the rate of technological change is associated with the availability of highly educated workers. Demographic structure and change support or inhibit economic growth.

As seen earlier, Group 2 is distinguished from other groups by many indicators. Group 2 has by far the highest mean GDP per capita, the highest economic growth rate, the lowest percentage of the labor force in agriculture, and the highest percentage of the labor force in industry and services. Group 1 ranks fifth in GDP per capita but second in the economic growth rate. Although primarily agricultural, this group has a substantial and growing industrial sector. Group 3 stays close to the middle ranking: third in GDP per capita, third in economic growth rate, and fifth in the percentage of labor in industry (Table 10).

Groups 4 and 5 are low-income agricultural countries, although Group 4 has a much larger proportion of labor force in industry. On nearly every indicator, Group 5 exhibits a wide range of values. Group 6 is comprised of nations with economic difficulty but relatively high education levels. Countries in Group 6 and socialist countries in Groups 1, 4, and 5 are, with differing rates of speed, moving from centralized or command economies to market economies (or socialist-market economies) which allow entrepreneurship and private capital formation. This transition for some Group 6 countries has resulted in negative economic growth. The rankings for Group 7 vary from second in GDP per capita to fifth in rate of economic growth.

The structure of a country's population provides one important context for understanding the growth of education systems and the constraints on support for economic growth. The size of the dependency ratio, i.e., of those population groups assumed to be less economically productive (typically age

Table 10: GDP per Capita Annual Growth Rates, 1985-1995

Group	Countries	Mean	Minimum	Maximum
1	2	5.75	3.20	8.30
2	4	6.10	4.80	7.70
3	5	3.94	1.20	8.40
4	2	(0.85)	(3.80)	2.10
5	2	2.55	2.40	2.70
6	3	(6.46)	(8.60)	(0.39)
7	1	2.30	2.30	2.30
Total	19	2.20	(8.60)	8.40

Note: Data in parentheses are negative.
Sources: UNESCO 1989, 1998.

groupings 0-14, and over 60 years of age), helps define the magnitude of social services, and, when large, has a moderating effect on economic growth. The dependency ratios of the 0-14 age groupings vary across DMCs from 19 percent in Hong Kong, China to 51 percent in the Marshall Islands. Groups of countries with high population growth rates and fertility rates, e.g., Groups 4, 5, and 7, have large percentages of population under age 15, suggesting a potential high demand for the early levels of education and constraint on efforts to improve education quality. The contribution of education to economic growth is generally found to be positive and significant when measured either in monetary terms or directly in terms of agricultural efficiency or labor productivity. Education also may contribute to poverty reduction, improvement in income distribution, and various dimensions of social, demographic, and political development. Although subject to some controversy, the relative significance of human capital has also been found to be generally stronger in less developed countries than in more developed countries (Psacharopoulos 1994; Tilak 1994, 1997).

Education at all levels contributes to economic growth through imparting attitudes and skills necessary for a variety of workplaces. Education also contributes to economic growth by improving health and reducing fertility, and – possibly – by contributing to political stability. Although the link between education and labor productivity is not entirely clear, general knowledge and learning skills acquired in school are usually assumed to make workers more capable of acquiring new skills and adapting to new working environments. The relevance of the education system to the labor market thus lies most fundamentally in its ability to produce a literate, disciplined, flexible labor force through a high-quality, universal basic education. As the economy continues to develop and new technology is applied to production, the demand for workers with more and better education increases. For example, countries with export-oriented industries have higher education requirements than those areas continuing with traditional agriculture and commerce. An example is the more industrialized coastal regions of the PRC, where lower secondary education plus language and computer skills are now required, as compared with inland regions where basic literacy suffices for traditional agricultural work.

A United Nations Development Programme (UNDP) report (1997, 97) observes that people who lack basic skills "cannot adapt to changing market conditions or shift to more sophisticated exports." The impact of globalization, integration of the world economy, deregulation of markets, technological change, migration of labor, and the rate of accumulation of new knowledge, all hasten the significant changes taking place in the technologies found in the labor markets in many countries, and impose new demands on education. The knowledge-intensive aspects of labor, now well-developed in a number of DMCs (most especially in Groups 2 and 3, but to some degree in all groups) require persons with the highest levels of technical and managerial competence. To respond to such needs, increasing differentiation is necessary at higher education levels, and availability of learning with different foci and at different ages. Advanced learning opportunities for economically advanced countries will mean high proportions of enrollments in science, industrial technology, information technology, and management.

The contrasting education and economic experiences of the NIEs and those of many of the other economies of South and Southeast Asia are striking. In the 1960s, all these economies were approximately at the same level of economic development. However, over the last three decades, growth in per capita incomes in East Asia has been about four times as fast as in South Asia. To some extent each nation sets its own priorities and follows its own route to development. Thus, the histories of those economies that have undergone sustained rapid economic growth may not represent the future of less developed nations. Nevertheless, a brief review of the education experiences of the NIEs can inform national and international discussions of education policies and practice, raise issues, and suggest directions and strategies worthy of examination.

The international research literature offers many, sometimes conflicting, reasons for the economic success of these economies. Supporting national policies have been stressed, including: outward-looking strategies; institutional reforms; land reforms; high-quality and merit-based economic technology; a reliable legal framework; political stability; savings and investment; good governance; demographic structure; and policy. Favorable demographic conditions identified include an increasing and relatively healthy labor force and a decreasing dependency ratio. Early and continued investment in education forming a satisfactory threshold level of human capital accumulation is also frequently cited as having a major impact on growth. In the view of the World Bank (1995), for example, primary education is the largest single contributor to the NIEs' economic growth rates. The NIEs tended to emphasize high-quality primary education accompanied by a largely self-financed university system. By contrast, as Haq (1997) points out, South Asian countries spent much of their small budgets on subsidies to higher levels of education.

The following is a summary of characteristics of NIEs prior to, or early in, the period of rapid economic growth:

- Every NIE as it entered its period of sustained economic growth already had in place a well-developed system of basic education that provided a minimum of six years of education for nearly all boys and girls. Some NIEs, e.g., the Republic of Korea and Taipei,China, had developed extensive secondary and higher education systems early in their industrialization.

- National commitment and political support for education was demonstrated in all the NIEs by enabling laws, national policies, and adequate central financing. Government expenditures on education were not, though, necessarily high prior to economic take-off, and in terms of education expenditures as a percentage of GNP, a significant variation can be found among NIEs. However, government efforts were often complemented by private education institutions and by significant financial and labor contributions from parents.

- At all levels of the government and education bureaucracies, including school, community, and family levels, there were high expectations for basic education. Teacher and pupil absenteeism was low, and teacher quality was comparatively high. The NIEs tended to be pragmatic and opportunistic in attempts to address problems of efficiency, quality, and equity in education. Innovations ran the technological gamut and covered a wide range of uses of personnel and facilities, including large classes. The education role of government in some NIEs, e.g., the Republic of Korea, changed incrementally as development proceeded. In the earlier period of growth, the central government acted essentially as a regulator, mandating changes and reforms. Subsequently, the government acted more as a facilitator, sponsoring and advocating exemplar programs.

- The record of NIEs in terms of provision of equal education opportunities to females has been mixed. Near-universal primary education for girls was quickly achieved. At higher levels of education, however, some disparity in enrollment rates persisted; and in post-school work opportunities, discriminatory practices favoring males remain the norm.

These rapidly growing economies have not been without educational, social, and economic problems. Educators in the NIEs are increasingly questioning the quality of their education systems. The human resources produced by the schools have learned to run the prevailing technology of development. The new education question is whether the schools can better assist in the acquisition of higher-order skills and creativity to sustain economic and social change. Moreover, at least some people are contemplating the price of recent successes. Visible along with the several attractive results of economic vitality are less attractive accompaniments, such as intergenerational contrasts in lifestyles and lack of communication, youth alienation and violence, intense competition for elite institutions, and overemphasis on consumerism. Nor has economic growth been a linear path upward. A variety of conditions, including global competition and bad investments and subsequent large debts by major industries, resulted in an economic downturn in the late 1990s.

Several attempts have been made to discern economic and education lessons from the experience of the NIEs. The macroeconomic policies and priority to human capital development have been applauded by international agencies and emulated by other Asian countries. A complete replication of the experience of any of the NIEs by another economy is, of course, impossible.

Education and Poverty Reduction

An old proverb observes that "a rising tide lifts all boats." Family income tends to be strongly associated with a reduction in the incidence of poverty. Likewise, economic growth is a powerful weapon against poverty, although growth does not necessarily eliminate poverty. As with education and economic growth, there is a two-way relationship between education and poverty. Family income is strongly positively associated with education attainment, and low earnings of the poor are the result partly of lower human capital endowments and partly of labor market discrimination (Quibria 1994). Reflecting the association of education and poverty, in the Philippines, data from 97 provinces and cities with provincial status demonstrated that the incidence of poverty was associated with the extent of school participation, frequency of school completion, and level and quality of school staffing.

Poverty reduces the opportunity for education attainment and acquisition of education outcomes, e.g., advanced education and preferred employment. Although data are lacking for many DMCs on percentages of population living in poverty, available data are consistent with other social and demographic indicators. For example, Group 5 has more than half its population in poverty, e.g., Nepal 53 percent, while for Group 3 the equivalent figure is 11.5 percent.

Many of the poor are women. Although no single profile suffices to describe women in poverty, many poor females live in villages, are not active in the labor force, are illiterate or have a low level of education, have few marketable skills, and, as women, are subject to discriminatory laws and traditions that inhibit their opportunities for equitable participation in employment. Conditions vary across and within country groupings, but no country has achieved full gender equity in the household, education system, and workplace. Indeed in Group 6, in countries that politically and economically are making a radical break with the past, a renewal of certain ethnic and religious traditions has been seen, accompanied by a reduction in female opportunities.

Women participate less than men in labor markets, and wage rates for females are consistently lower than those for males. Women constitute the majority of unpaid family workers. Some increases in female labor force participation rates can be found in several Asian economies and can be attributed to several factors, including social and cultural transformations in societies that have altered women's attitudes; economic development; changes in family structure; and increases in education. Given the conditions of limited labor force involvement, self-employment may be the only realistic option for many urban women and men. Policies thus are needed to improve the productivity of self-employed and unpaid family workers as well as efforts to create more employment opportunities to become wage workers. Although the link between education and employment is often tenuous, provision of schooling is one approach to the creation and distribution of new individual and family wealth. Schooling thus contributes to the reduction of absolute and relative poverty. However, these influences of education do not take effect until the poor begin to earn more or become self-employed, and consume more effectively – changes that may require a generation. Moreover, the marginal individual benefits of additional schooling when relatively few complete schooling tend to be greater than when graduation ratios are high. Additionally a debate persists on the relative value of general education and specific skill training, e.g., entrepreneurship and basic accounting, for the urban informal sector (Lee 2002).

Laws and policies supportive of equal opportunities for girls and women in the workplace are critically important but may not be sufficient to alter inhibiting gender traditions and culture. Governments and international agencies committed to gender equity need vigorously to encourage equitable employ-ment conditions at all institutional levels from the family to the state. Within the education sector, strategies are necessary to promote more women to decision-making roles.

Education, Social Change, and Social Cohesion

New, broader definitions of development have emerged. In addition to traditional economic measures, another language and new concepts have entered the discourse on national development. The newer terms include poverty reduction, social justice, environmental sustainability, human rights, and, at times, empowerment. This extended conceptualization of development is being translated into a larger range of policies and programs to address new human and social dimensions. This change is recognized by international agencies whose priorities increasingly focus on improving individual compe-tencies and building institutional capacities rather than focusing only on physical infrastructure.

Social changes may be seen as integral to, prerequisite to, or a conse-quence of, economic development. The effects of industrialization and globalization are making changes at the individual, family, and workplace levels. Gender has emerged internationally as a social and political issue, and questions are being asked by those concerned with gender equity as to what rules govern access to, and control over, resources and labor, and how definitions of rules, rights, and obligations are reinforced and on occasion, openly challenged.

Information and education are two ingredients for helping individuals and institutions participate in social change. Countries that rank comparatively high in terms of circulation of newspapers and television sets per 1,000 population tend to be more economically and educationally advanced. Among DMCs, circulation of daily newspapers per 1,000 inhabitants is extremely low in all groups with the exception of Group 2. Groups 1, 3, 4, 5, 6, and 7 cluster as a group distinct from Group 2 with a daily circulation ranging from 5.5 to 62.3, while Group 2 has a daily circulation of an average 407.2 newspapers per

Education and National Development

1,000 inhabitants. Circulation is especially low in Group 5 with a maximum of 8 and in Group 6 with a maximum of 11 newspapers. Groups 2 and 6 rank at the top for number of television sets per 1,000 inhabitants. Groups 4 and 5 cluster at the lower end, but other groups exhibit a large standard deviation and a wide range, indicating considerable variation within each group.

The social objectives for education are commonly ambitious, and may include:

- developing among students a critical orientation toward institutions and social problems;
- eliminating discrimination and reducing elitism;
- promoting national unity;
- learning to work cooperatively with others;
- resolving conflicts nonviolently; and
- developing self-reliance.

National and family education objectives suggest that learning should be more than examination results on standardized achievement tests. Such tests at best measure a small fraction of acquired knowledge, and relate little to many of the values, beliefs, and traditions that families and societies wish to perpetuate. Education may be seen as a source of self-development or of skills to cope with a wide variety of external problems, including the productivity of labor. As education systems develop, the education process may be expected to turn its attention to higher-order goals such as problem solving and creativity, which themselves are processes, and which are seen as more enduring and widely applicable forms of learning.

Major education changes and reforms reflect the social, cultural, religious, and political contexts and traditions of particular countries. Extensions of the length of basic education and responses to demand for secondary and higher education are often stimulated as much by motivation to build political capital as by concern for improved human capital. However, education changes are also initiated through the regular processes of particular education bureaucracies in their attempts to adapt and improve the functioning of education systems.

Formal education cannot eliminate problems associated with social and economic change, nor even fully prepare the population to cope with these changes. However, an effective and equitable system of formal and nonformal education can promote intergroup parity (rural-urban, gender), develop shared appreciations, bring home and school closer together, and increase at the community level the sharing of decisions affecting youth. Carnoy (1995) suggests that there are two opposing social views of education. One stresses capital accumulation and the other social equality. He suggests that there is an inherent conflict between schooling's role in preparing labor for a modernizing economy and its role in equalizing opportunities and providing social opportunity.

Carnoy's analysis may be valid, and much of the international literature defends the priority accorded to basic education on the grounds of its contribution to productivity. However, shifts in priority from higher to lower levels of education can also be defended on equity and cultural grounds such as social mobility. Emphasis on basic education helps the lowest income groups gain education and social access. This priority further allows the targeting of remote areas and ignored populations.

Teaching and Learning: Inside the Black Box

Improvements in the quality – and to some extent the efficiency and equity – of education depend on the nexus of teaching and learning. The characteristics, meanings, and effects of the interaction of teachers and students cannot be mandated from central offices of ministries of education. Schooling – the formal teaching-learning environment – is to some extent a self-contained system, and different schools (or even classrooms) may respond to given sets of inputs in different ways. This section examines the dimensions of effective teaching and learning within the school, and its immediate external relations with parents and communities.

Although attempts to measure learning within and outside school settings take place in all DMCs, comparative cross-country data on student achievement are rare. The studies by the International Association for the Evaluation of Educational Achievement (IEA) of science learning include data from Hong Kong, China; Republic of Korea; Papua New Guinea; Philippines; Singapore; Taipei,China; and Thailand, along with data from 13 other economies (Postlethwaite and Wiley 1992). The results show that for the 14-year-old international population samples, the Republic of Korea and Taipei,China ranked fifth and seventh, respectively; Singapore and Thailand 14th and 15th; and Papua New Guinea and Hong Kong, China 18th and 19th. In the pre-university sample the positions changed: Hong Kong, China ranked first or second for each of the three main science subjects, with Singapore close behind. The performance of the Republic of Korea overlapped with Thailand's, ranked between 13th and 15th. Singapore and Hong Kong, China both have very selective systems, which partly explains their superior performance at the pre-university level. Those taking science in these economies are a much more selected group than in the Republic of Korea. These assessments confirm that the performance of 13-year-olds in science in the Republic of Korea is better than in most developed countries in the study, as is that of Taipei,China and the PRC samples. In mathematics, similar patterns appear with the same economies performing at the highest ranks.

Many of the policy documents published by the World Bank and ADB seek to specify inputs that determine academic achievement and knowledge skills that translate directly into increased productivity of labor. Tables 11 and 12 summarize two bodies of research related to the determinants of school outputs, typically measured by scores on standardized achievement tests. Table 11 presents the findings of a number of studies of school effects in Asia using a production function or input-output model. The available studies are few, and generalizations to all DMCs are not possible. However, the contradictions among the findings are striking. Table 12 summarizes a body of literature known as "effective schools research." Although this research, in terms of variables examined, overlaps with the studies referred to in Table 11, somewhat more attention is given to school process variables (Chapman and Adams 2002).

The advantage of the input-output studies as reported in Table 11 is that a policymaker is shown a number of manipulable variables or conditions around which intervention strategies may be developed. Although many studies of school effects have been carried out in a number of Asian countries, they are rarely comparable. Studies on noncomparable populations in different time periods in Indonesia suggest some improvement in equality over the last few decades (Moegiadi 1976; Suryadi 1989). There are, however, two major weaknesses of such studies as a basis for education policy. First, the inconsistency of findings rarely offers a clear, unequivocal direction as to which inputs should have priority. Second, the input-output (production function) model on which these studies are based radically oversimplifies the dynamic and situation-specific nature of teaching-learning processes.

Table 12 summarizes the second body of relevant research, i.e., effective schools research, and captures many of the organizational and process variables found in these studies. Because of the general, and sometimes vague, nature of several of these dimensions, e.g., positive school climate and effective use of instructional time, the research cannot easily be used to develop more effective schools. Moreover, the research on effective schools, largely carried out in Europe and North America, shares many of the weaknesses of school-effects studies: lack of underlying theory, methodological weaknesses, and lack of consistency of findings. The summary of conditions of effective schools shown in Table 12 is one of many that could have been developed from available research.

In developing viable and dynamic education systems, a major priority is the creation of a sustainable learning environment of acceptable quality. Teachers and teaching shape the quality of learning. However, research offers limited policy direction regarding how much should be invested in which kinds of training. As shown in Tables 11 and 12, some scattered research attempts to determine which teacher inputs improve student learning. However, the findings are inconsistent across countries and require much caution as a basis for policy. There is not, for example, a consistent relationship between years of formal education, extent of preservice and in-service training, education expenditures, class size, and student performance.

Other apparent solutions to improvements of teaching and learning turn out to be complex because of organizational context. For example, teacher motivation is widely assumed to be a contributing factor to improved instruction and learning. Frequently suggested incentives include (i) merit pay to motivate teachers with a significant portion of a teachers' salary based on performance as assessed by supervisors; (ii) salary premiums to mathematics and science teachers; and (iii) location premiums to teachers working in rural areas (Chapman 2002).

Table 11: Selected Studies of School Effects in Asian Economies

Study	Economy	Findings	Source
School expenditures per pupil	Malaysia (secondary)	Higher school expenditures are not associated with higher achievement.	Beebout 1972
	Thailand	Textbook expenditures raise the national academic achievement.	Heyneman and Jamison 1984
Class size	Thailand	Negative evidence that small class size improves student achievement in reading and science.	Heyneman and Loxley 1983
	India	No evidence that smaller class size raises achievement.	Heyneman and Loxley 1983
	Malaysia (secondary)	Fewer students per teacher improve the quality of interaction and raise achievement.	Beebout 1972
	Indonesia (secondary)	No evidence that smaller class size improves student achievement.	Sembiring and Livingstone 1981
	Indonesia (primary)	Class size has negative effects on student achievement.	Moegiadi 1976
School size	Thailand	School size does affect student achievement.	Comber and Keeves 1973
	Malaysia (primary)	Large school size has negative effect on student achievement.	Beebout 1972
Instructional materials	India	Greater availability of instructional materials leads to higher student achievement in reading and science.	Comber and Keeves 1973
	Philippines	Instructional materials do impact on student achievement in science.	Heyneman et al. 1983
	Indonesia (secondary)	No evidence that instructional materials lead to higher student achievement.	Sembiring and Livingstone 1981
	Thailand (primary)	Instructional materials do not improve student achievement.	Fuller and Chantavanish 1976
	Malaysia (primary)	Instructional materials do matter in student achievement.	Haron 1977
School library	India, Thailand	The presence and active use of a school library raise achievement.	Thorndike 1973
	Malaysia (primary and secondary)	Ditto.	Haron 1977
	Indonesia (secondary)	The availability and use of a library do not improve student achievement.	Beebout 1972; Sembiring et al. 1981
Laboratories	India (primary), Iran, Thailand	The presence and instructional time spent in laboratories raise science achievement.	Heyneman and Loxley 1983
School feeding programs	Thailand	Malnutrition lowers student achievement.	Fuller and Chantavanish 1976
Teacher experience	India, Iran, Malaysia (secondary)	Teachers with longer experience improve student achievement.	Beebout 1972; Heyneman and Loxley 1983
	Malaysia (primary)	Ditto.	Haron 1977
	Indonesia	No evidence that teacher experience is associated with student achievement.	Sembiring et al. 1981
Preservice teacher training	India	Teachers' years of schooling raise student achievement.	Comber and Keeves 1973; Heyneman and Loxley 1983

Education and National Development

Study	Economy	Findings	Source
	Thailand, India, Iran	Teachers' years of post-secondary instruction lead to higher student performance.	Beebout 1972
	Malaysia (primary)	Ditto.	Haron 1977
	Indonesia (secondary)	Teachers' years of schooling do not affect student achievement.	Sembiring et al. 1981
In-service teacher training	Indonesia	Upgrading the skills of teachers leads to higher student achievement.	Sembiring and Livingstone 1981
Length of instruction	India, Thailand	More hours or days of instruction increase student achievement.	Heyneman and Loxley 1983
Homework	India, Thailand	No evidence that homework raises student achievement.	Comber and Keeves 1973
High teacher expectation	Hong Kong, China; Thailand	Teachers who expect high achievement raise student performance.	Fuller and Chantavanish 1976; Rowe et al. 1966
Teacher's time spent on class	India, Iran	More hours spent preparing for class raises student achievement.	Heyneman and Loxley 1983
	Thailand	No evidence that class preparation leads to higher student achievement.	Heyneman and Loxley 1983
Active teaching and learning	Indonesia (primary)	Students participating in active learning perform better than students without active learning.	Tangyong 1989
Principal salary	Indonesia (secondary)	Higher salaries attract stronger principals, improve the instructional programs, and raise achievement.	Sembiring and Livingstone 1981
Number of class shifts	Malaysia (secondary)	More than one shift of classes each day strains the effectiveness of resources and lowers achievement.	Beebout 1972
Student boarding	Malaysia	Living in school does not ensure that student achievement will be raised.	Beebout 1972
Student repetition	Thailand	Holding low-achieving students at a grade level will boost academic performance.	Fuller and Chantavanish 1976
Vocational curriculum	Indonesia, Philippines, Thailand	Vocational curriculum is negatively associated with an effective labor force and earnings.	Clark 1983; Psacharopoulos 1973
In-plant vocational training	Korea, Rep. of	In-plant training is more cost effective.	Lee 1985
Preprimary schooling	Thailand (primary)	Third graders who attended preprimary schools performed better in math and Thai language than did children who had no preprimary experience.	Raudenbush 1991
Status of parents	Nepal	Parents' socioeconomic status significantly determines school access of children.	Shresta et al. 1986
Gender differences	Indonesia, Malaysia	Both girls and boys demonstrate favorable attitude toward math and possess equivalent problem-solving skills.	Swetz et al. 1991

Source: Consolidated by Muhammad, H. 1998.

Table 12: Dimensions of Effective Schooling

Dimensions	Core elements	Facilitating elements
Leadership	• Positive climate and overall atmosphere • School and classroom site management and decision making • Strong leadership • Goal-focused activities toward clear, attainable, and relevant objectives • Planned and coordinated curriculum • School-wide staff development • Consistency of school values	• Shared consensus on values and goals • Long-range planning and coordination • Stability and continuity of key staff • District-level support for school improvement
Efficacy	• High and positive achievement expectation with a constant press for excellence • Visible rewards for academic excellence and growth • Cooperative activity and group interaction in the classroom • Total staff involvement with school improvement • Autonomy and flexibility to implement adaptive practices • Appropriate levels of difficulty for learning tasks • Teacher empathy, rapport, and personal interaction with students	• Emphasis on homework and study • Positive accountability acceptance of responsibility for learning outcomes • Strategies to avoid nonpromotion of students • De-emphasis of strict ability grouping • Interaction with more accomplished peers • Sense of school community • Parental involvement and support
Efficiency	• Effective use of instructional time: amount and intensity of engagement in school learning • Orderly and disciplined school and classroom environment • Continuous diagnosis, evaluation, and feedback • Intellectually challenging teaching • Well-structured classroom activities • Instruction guided by content coverage • School-wide emphasis on basic and higher-order skills • Pupil acceptance of school norms	• Positive teacher models • Opportunities for individualized work • Number and variety of opportunity to learn • School-wide recognition of academic success

In addition to the lack of consistency in research findings and the impreciseness of the dimensions of effectiveness, one difficulty in suggesting strategies for improvements in instruction is that in much important learning there may be a lack of linear order. That is, the usual interpretation of increases in learning being directly associated with time on task, and the usual fixed sequence of teaching suggested in lesson plans, for example, may not be relevant to an approach to progressive, constructive, interactive learning. Again, the level of current insight into the complexities of teaching and learning suggests that the best strategy lies in experimentation, careful monitoring, and feedback.

Unfortunately, in practice none of these is guaranteed to work. Teachers who do not receive merit pay may respond not by trying harder but rather by reducing their effort. And, paying premium salaries to mathematics and science teachers may make other teachers angry, frustrated, and bitter. Further, teachers apparently would rather be unemployed in urban areas than work in certain remote regions (Murnane and Cohen 1986).

As a second example, the importance of strong school management to teaching, learning, and effective schools is well established. Yet experiments in site-based management often do not produce significant change in teaching and learning. Visible changes are not always welcomed by neighboring or competing schools, and leadership over time requires multiple advocates. The lesson is that school-level efforts at reform are fragile, and may not survive if not reinforced by community or regional support.

There is potentially an important role for national standards to play in improving teaching and learning. National standards with sufficient supporting resources for teacher familiarization and training can have a powerful impact on national education quality. They are effective, however, only to the extent that they are integrated with curriculum, textbooks, and the continuing professional development of teachers. Sustaining such integrated reforms may require changes in school management and in how schools relate to families and communities. If agreement can be reached on standards for student achievement and their assessment, and if the standards are made a priority in schools all over the country, then the groundwork is laid for systemic change.

The lack of compelling research findings, and the often contradictory evidence culled from experience, stresses the need for caution. However, the potential for improving the teaching-learning process is not as bleak as the inconsistencies in research and complexities of practice may suggest. Research and critical examination of practice do offer insights sufficient to initiate small- and larger-scale interventions viewed as experiments. Research on school effects and effective schools offers significant insights that could become part of in-service training programs for teachers and principals or for district or school cluster-level experiments. Strategies to improve teaching and learning are likely to include:

- improving school management;
- increasing learning materials and instructional time;
- upgrading subject matter knowledge and pedagogic skills; and
- encouraging parental and community involvement in developing a supportive learning environment.

Additional characteristics of effective teaching and learning might involve establishing high expectations for students and, at all levels of schooling, including explicit attempts to integrate work knowledge and skills into the curriculum.

Research and experience indicate that much remains to be learned about the contents of the black box. This lack of knowledge stresses the importance of experimentation with new curricula and new delivery mechanisms. One problem is that the poorest countries and poorest education systems, which arguably need innovations and cost-effective teaching and learning the most, have the least capital to invest for such purposes. More insight needs to be acquired by examining cases of successes and failures at the community and school level (Chapman 2002). Why, for example, in some communities is there decline in demand for schooling? Why do some communities reject existing schools? What unwanted outcomes do parents fear?

Policies, Issues, and Trends by Subsystem

Well described, largely in the documents produced by agencies involved in international assistance such as the World Bank and ADB, is a convergence of opinions on appropriate general priorities and broad strategies for education in support of economic growth and social equity. The recommended policy directions, although not without controversy, tend to emphasize:

- universal basic education;
- privatization and public-private partnerships, particularly in secondary, higher, and vocational/technical education;
- special attention to girls' and women's education;
- decentralization, or at least the transfer of some of the activities of education planning and reform from the center to lower echelons of government;
- teacher and administrator professionalization; and
- the search for multiple sources and channels for the financing of education.

Embedded within, and cutting across these priority recommendations are pervasive policy and operational concerns with:

- systemic, organizational, and classroom-level improvements in education quality;
- the promotion of equity in supply and delivery of education for all children and youth;
- increasing managerial effectiveness, and raising institutional capabilities at all levels of education systems; and
- developing and effectively utilizing multiple and new sources of financing.

Although the general rationale for the new policies and practices is clear and often persuasive, the precise nature of necessary reforms is often less clear. Recommended policies and priorities for education are often sketched in only general terms, with necessary supporting environmental conditions only partly considered; the constraints on implementation and utilization of new programs are rarely examined in depth. A major task for policymakers, planners, researchers, and international agencies is to unbundle these broad strategies and give them meaning within particular contexts. In this process of clarification, specification, and implementation of actions, at issue is the role of international agencies.

Preprimary Education

A substantial body of research suggests that preprimary and early childhood education can have a strong, positive influence on success in subsequent schooling. Such education may be particularly effective in reducing subsequent primary school dropout rates among the poor. Preprimary education in DMCs is largely private, often delivered in a highly informal manner, and susceptible to economic conditions. Group 6 countries reflect this, where the transition to a market economy has had very negative effects on preprimary education.

A number of cases of intersectoral cooperation among DMCs include components of preprimary and early childhood education. One successful case is reported from the Philippines (Box 2).

Basic Education

The nearly universal priority status given to basic education is based on a belief that all children, irrespective of whether they continue in schooling or enter the world of work, need literacy, numeracy, and citizenship skills. As employment moves from agriculture to industry, and the population from rural to urban areas, basic education gains in importance. As enrollment rates approach 100 percent, priorities move further from access to quality. Decentralization impacts especially on basic education since this subsector is most likely to come under local responsibility. The uncertainty of quality of local leadership, the fragility of funding, the search for cost-effective quality, changing managerial roles at all levels, and the incompleteness of information for decisions may combine to constrain local education development.

Primary or basic education, because of its crucial function within the education system and contributions to economic growth, is given highest priority by major international agencies. All of the educationally less developed DMCs appear to accept this priority. High-quality basic schooling lays the foundation for further academic or vocational education, contributes basic competencies to the labor force, and improves the ability to learn. In turn, these factors contribute to productivity both in the household and in the market. One dominant view is that vocational and technical education and training are most effective when they follow a sound general education and are job related.

This view also suggests that a strong background in primary and secondary education provides individuals with a bigger chance of obtaining and profiting by in-service training.

Two major questions, however, concern what is meant by basic education and how relevant is the form in which it is delivered. If "basic" implies the fundamental knowledge and skills necessary in a changing economy and society, then as technological change and the means of production become more sophisticated, people need different and more advanced "basic" skills.

Box 2: Integrated Early Education and Development – The Philippines

One program which demonstrates collaboration among parents, teachers, and local government in planning and improving education service delivery is the Naga Early Education and Development (NEED) program, in the Philippines. The program addresses three concerns of Naga City:

- The devolution of Department of Social Welfare and Development (DSWD) functions to local government units pursuant to the Local Government Code;
- The increasing demand for better day care services by the local populace, which was triggered by the emergence of costly and mostly inaccessible privately owned preschool centers; and
- The evident need for quality services for the often-neglected handicapped sectors.

The NEED program has several innovative features. First, it has a strong partnership between program initiators and partners. Second, it has enhanced capabilities of local programs that guaranteed better access to quality education, impelled greater parental participation in early education, and bolstered the government's Moral Recovery Program by targeting the very young. Third, its focus on the handicapped created awareness of the plight of the neglected disabled sector of society, and provided a means for the mainstreaming of handicapped children. Finally, the program can easily be replicated in other government units.

The NEED program has the following components: (i) Survey for Early Detection of Developmental and Congenital Anomalies, (ii) Montessori System, (iii) School for Early Education and Development, (iv) HELP Learning Center, and (v) Special Education Program. The program starts with the enumeration of children with and without disabilities. Placement is either with the special education center and HELP Learning Centers which cater to special children or the School for Early Education and Development or the Montessori System which serves children without disabilities. The NEED program "programs" the child for admission into the formal elementary system.

The program caters to the 27 sitios of Naga with 60 barangay Montessori-type day care centers. It serves children aged 3-5 years regardless of their socioeconomic status or their mental and physical condition. The program has 72 staff, among whom 55 are part-time volunteers, 10 are full-time permanent employees, and six are co-terminus officers.

The cost is shared by the local government unit which provides a monthly honorarium of P800 per teacher, the barangay council which supplements the local government unit honoraria and provides center facilities, and parents who donate a voluntary amount monthly.

Source: Manugue et al. 1997.

Likewise, to participate fully in a changing civil society, higher communication and analytical skills are needed. Further, basic education, whether at the primary or secondary level, typically teaches numeracy and literacy abstracted from their use. Schooling makes a sharp division between knowledge (knowing what) and practice (knowing how and when), and the culture of the school contrasts with the culture of the work environment. The separation of the "theory" as offered in basic education and practice from application in the real world raises questions about both the meaningfulness of instruction and the relevance to the external environment. These observations suggest that there is room for experimentation with alternative approaches to delivery of basic skills and understandings.

Junior Secondary Education

Junior secondary education is already a part of basic education in several DMCs, and is projected to be an integral part of basic education within 15 years in several more. Extending compulsory or universal education to nine years is a landmark decision in the development of education systems. It suggests an education commitment equivalent to many industrialized and modernized societies throughout the world. However, among DMCs such a redefinition of basic education has not necessarily altered the curriculum or instructional patterns of either primary or junior secondary schools. The major challenges to planners and policymakers are to integrate junior secondary education into an articulated basic education as necessary, maintain its integration with upper levels of education, and provide options for the range of needs for a diverse student population. The need for the content of basic education to be responsive to its context is illustrated by the changing skills and knowledge needed as agriculture shifts from a low to high technology base. Table 13 suggests that the minimum learning requirements for participation in the agriculture sector are quite different as the sector increases its productivity through technology and planning. Could existing basic education programs meet the challenge of Level D (see Table 13)?

Senior Secondary Education

The major issue at the senior secondary level relates to the appropriate curriculum mix between general and specific skills. At this level, education becomes increasingly specialized; many DMCs have had a continuing debate over the appropriate extent of its vocationalization. Providing an academic curriculum is the least expensive approach, and in many countries appears to offer equal or better employment opportunities than existing vocational tracks. As an alternative to skills-oriented programs, a new curriculum innovation, called technology education, is being experimented with internationally and is a subject of discussion in East and Southeast Asian countries. Technology education is a synthetic course or program which seeks to develop under-standing of applied science and mathematics in the context of technological changes. This approach is cheaper and requires less equipment than pure vocational programs.

The demand for secondary schooling depends on the objectives attributed to this level of schooling by parents and students, the behavior of the labor market, and the financial capability of parents. Rapidly expanding

Table 13: Four Basic Stages of Agricultural Productivity and their Learning Requirements

Agricultural levels	Former entrepreneurs' technology level	Agricultural inputs	Minimum learning requirements
Level A	Traditional farming techniques passed from parent to child.	Local varieties of seeds and implements.	Addition and subtraction – not necessarily acquired through formal education.
Level B	Intermediate technology.	Small quantities of fertilizer.	Addition, subtraction, division, and rudimentary literacy.
Level C	Fully improved technology.	High-yielding varieties: proven seeds, rate of application of seed, fertilizer, and pest control per acre.	Multiplication, long division, and other more complex mathematical procedures; reading and writing abilities, and rudimentary knowledge of chemistry and biology.
Level D	Full irrigation-based farming.	All above inputs: tubewell access during the off-season, and water rates per acre.	Mathematics, independent written communication, high reading comprehension, ability to research unfamiliar words and concepts; elementary chemistry, biology, physics; and regular access to information from print and electronic sources.

Source: Heyneman 1997.

enrollments often outstrip the number of new jobs being created. However, the substantial cost of senior secondary schools simply prices this level of education out of reach for many poor. Demand is also reduced because certain types of industry seek young unskilled workers for menial jobs.

Faced with increasing output of junior secondary education and an emerging demand for upper secondary education, countries are beginning to look for alternative avenues for post-basic education. In the short-term future, one strand of senior secondary education will remain focused on academic preparation for higher education. In addition to an academic program, experimentation may be expected with a wide variety of vocational schooling and training arrangements that allow transferability and easy entrance and exit. The general assumption among researchers and policymakers appears to be that academic schooling is most effective for learning of more general conceptual and cultural knowledge. The workplace apparently is most effective for work-related knowledge (cognitive models of tasks and devices) and work-related skills (procedural, social, cultural).

Tertiary Education

The next decade will likely bring expansion of tertiary education in DMCs, increased privatization, increased differentiation within higher education systems, and more attention to the quality of instruction and research. The direction of policies in higher education is toward development of more competitive and productive institutions supported by one or more public or private sources, with increasing autonomy in determining the composition of the student body and curriculum. This direction of policy does not necessarily eliminate the need for appropriate government regulatory frameworks, accreditation, and public subsidies.

In order to attain increased flexibility and efficiency in meeting the social demands and education needs of the economy, policymakers in higher education will seek:

- more efficient use of public funds;
- increasing reliance on students' families for financing a high proportion of costs;
- increased fees in public institutions;
- linkage between public support and measures of productivity; and
- direct profit-making activities by universities and higher technical institutions, often in collaboration with private industry.

Considering these funding adjustments, a basic equity question will need to be addressed: Does shifting the financial burden to students, as implied by cost sharing, in fact decrease equity in the delivery of higher education? Does this, in turn, contribute to increasing the education gap between the richest and poorest citizens?

Implementation of major changes toward institutional autonomy, self-governance, and market orientation will be difficult for several reasons. First, there is a tradition for faculty and staff to be perceived as civil servants with implied employment constraints. Second, in socialist and former socialist states, higher education was developed essentially as a model of specialized, usually mono-disciplinary universities. And third, moving control to the private sector or to nongovernment management boards may be difficult because it decreases the role of the state in enrollment and the curriculum.

The Changing Pattern of Policy and Planning

Major changes, often encouraged by international agencies, are taking place in education governance among most DMCs. In varying degrees, at different speeds and following a range of paths, there is growing devolution of education responsibilities and, in some cases, decision authority. This general trend can have profound effects on the actors in education decisions: the strategies for change; the opportunities for localizing curricula; the operational meaning given to such concepts as quality, efficiency and relevance in education; and how education services are financed. These changes may have equally profound effects on the direction and content of the roles of international agencies.

This section analyzes the issues and trends in education governance, most particularly the trends of evolution of the structure of policy making[2] and planning. Two country case studies of somewhat different approaches to devolution of education decisions are described. The potential benefits and risks are identified, and the conditions necessary for sustaining cycles of planning, monitoring, knowledge utilization, and education improvement are explored.

Decentralization and Localization

Although experimentation with community development has historically been widespread, policy making and planning among DMCs are functions typically associated with central governments. The formal responsibilities for development of major policies and comprehensive planning legally or by tradition frequently reside with the national legislature and within ministries of education, finance, and planning. Based on the assumption that policy is primarily an activity of senior officials in the central bureaucracies, international

---

[2] The term 'policy' is used in many different ways. Policy can refer to a law, a binding government decision, a set of goals, an organizational commitment, or a general strategy. Policy making, as the process of determining policy, depends on the definition of policy. Given the several meanings of policy, the term policymaker could refer to legislation, government officials, various education organizations, administrators, or teachers. Discussion here assumes that policy implies an authoritative statement or set of guidelines involving government or legal bodies and subject to enforcement. Because of the legal or formal connotations of the term policy, some governments, when describing sanctioned education reforms or changes, prefer to use the term 'strategy'. Education policy making, as the term is used here, is typically a process of making major education choices and setting directions for the education system or one or more subsectors. It is an intensely political process involving high-ranking bureaucrats, elected officials, and a variety of concerned groups. The transparency of the process varies across governments and cultures. It is customary to distinguish between the processes of policy formulation and policy implementation, although in practice the demarcation is often unclear.

agencies have given much attention to technical assistance and capacity building projects designed to inform and support policymakers in their work.

The shift in the processes and locus of control of policy and planning in education in DMCs is well under way in several countries and at an initial stage in others. The motivations for movement of education decisions away from the center reflect dissatisfaction with existing centralized systems. The objectives include:

- to find an alternative or addition to central government financing because of insufficient central resources, by requiring local governments to share financial responsibilities and develop private support;
- to improve efficiency of education as part of a general movement toward market-based development strategies that replace central planning;
- to increase the efficiency, relevance, and effectiveness of education by encouraging participation of parents and the community; and
- to reflect new models of planning and decision making which, for purposes of increased relevance and improved quality, emphasize wider participation and collaboration.

Decentralization[3] is generally related to the granting of some of the national government's authority to lower level units with the implication that local institutions can be developed that are, to a degree, autonomous from the central government. Decentralization typically further implies the right to develop local resources to be utilized at local discretion, thereby strengthening local government units financially and legally.

Table 14 summarizes the status of education governance in eight DMCs. Two cases, the PRC and India, are described below in more detail.

Table 14: Cross-Country Comparisons of Education Decentralization

Country	Center	Province	District	Village
PRC	Macro management or macro guidance. As part of a decentralization program, the central government developed a financial responsibility system that authorized the raising of funds at each of the local, provincial, and central levels.	Implements national laws, regulations, and policies; length of schooling, yearly enrollment selection of textbooks, number of teachers, and teaching salaries.	Within national guidelines responsibilities determined by provincial government. Local governments permitted to raise resources through various forms of taxation.	Community education committees generate funds and material assistance; engage in macro management of schools: supervision and assessment; encourage community participation.
Indonesia	Beginning dialogue on development of a more limited role emphasizing the establishment of regulations, setting standards, evaluation.	Coordination of implementation of policy on basic education. Partner with the center in planning and	Beginning of dialogue on steps to improve planning and management capacity at the district level. Consideration	

---

[3] Terms frequently used in discussing decentralization include localization, individualization, devolution, democratization, deconcentration, debureaucratization, and privatization.

Country	Center	Province	District	Village
		managing teacher training; mediator between education authority in district level and MOEC.	of training local expertise.	
Kyrgyz Republic	Establish national policies, plans, and programs; develop legal and legislative base for education; develop and maintain national R&D; provision of national standards, testing, and certification.	Region: Gradual assumption of responsibilities for regional planning, standards, and finance; coordination of associations and groups involved in education.		
Nepal	The Planning Commission sets guidelines for broad national policy and planning providing the Ministry of Education overall education development directions. The Ministry of Education drafts national policies and plans, coordinates the national-level programs, and conducts monitoring and evaluation.	Region: The Regional Education Directorate (RED) coordinates, monitors and evaluates programs at the regional level. RED has the authority to recruit teachers at the secondary level.	The 75 districts through the District Education Office (DEO) are the implementing units and district-level coordinating, monitoring, and evaluation units. Each district has an education committee representing community organizations, parents, and head teachers. The committee reviews district-level programs.	The School Management Committee (SMC), consisting of an elected local chairman and representatives from parents, oversees school development activities and approves programs to be forwarded to the DEO. The SMC raises local funds in support of the school and mobilizes the community for other school assistance.
Pakistan	The federal government is responsible for national policies and programs for all social sectors including education. The federal Ministry of Education (MoE) sets policy standards, develops curriculum, prepares national plans and budgets (with the Ministry of Finance). MoE further acts as a technical resource and as a channel of communication on national education policy to the provinces.	The province has primary responsibility for implementing education plans and programs, and formulates provincial policies, regulations, and procedures. Primary education management through separate directorates. Production of textbooks.	The provinces are divided into divisions and further subdivided into districts (districts are divided into talukas and tehsils). The district has authority to recruit teachers and select school sites.	Village education management committees manage day-to-day school activities.
Philippines	Formulation of policies, strategic planning, and budget preparation; development of standards for facilities, curriculum and teachers; R&D; monitoring and program assessment.	Region: Technical assistance in local instructional and program improvement; monitoring and evaluation of Division office; budget coordination;	Organization of school-based in-service training, organization of textbooks and materials' distribution system in district; general administration	

Country	Center	Province	District	Village
		management training of principals and supervisors. <u>Division</u>: Policy implementation; division strategic planning; program development and implementation; instructional supervision; monitoring and evaluation of district and school performance.	support to schools; management of district-level indicator systems.	
Papua New Guinea	Foundational policies for all levels of education, curriculum development; teacher training, examinations, and certification; planning and professional support to provinces; organizing supply of textbooks; management of tertiary institutions and national high schools; mobilization of funds and donor liaison.	Development of policies on school fees; implementation of provincial education plans; data collection for national-level ordering and distribution of textbooks and materials; appointment of secondary level teachers; teachers' salaries; financial aspects of capital works; operation and maintenance costs.		Responsible at primary and elementary levels for: nonsalary budgeting for operation and maintenance; maintenance of teachers' houses; expansion and maintenance of adult literacy.
Viet Nam	The Ministry of Education and Training has major responsibility for policy formation, national examinations, directing and inspecting all education curricula, and managing directly more than 40 universities. Other ministries also control and manage various kinds of education institutions. Central education authorities act as a redistribution mechanism when local resources are insufficient.	The provinces operate college-level institutions (established to meet local human resources demand) and all secondary schools. Eighty percent of the general education budget is paid from local resources (province and below).	The districts manage primary and lower secondary schools. (Much of the support for these schools come through mobilizing local resources.) Local contributions cover much of the expenditures on building construction, teachers' salaries, and school fees.	All schools have an association of parents and students. Parents are asked to pay more of the costs of education.

MOEC: Ministry of Education and Culture.
Source: Information from ADB Country Sector Studies.

The PRC Case

From 1949 to 1978, the PRC was characterized by highly centralized policy making, planning, and administration. Local governments with little discretion implemented central policies. In the late 1970s, as part of a broad program of economic and fiscal reform, the PRC developed new policies affecting education governance and designed to stimulate provinces to maximize their efforts for revenue collection. A major objective was to test the capabilities of management of townships, particularly to test the potential of rural areas to raise funds and accept responsibility for managing primary and middle schools.

An important early step in education decentralization in the PRC was taken when in 1985 the Ministry of Education became the State Education Commission (SEdC) with increased powers for coordination of all ministerial efforts in education. Education decentralization took the form of administrative and financial devolution, with emphasis on the latter. Diversification in education funding required mobilization of local sources to be supplemented by central government subsidies. Further provided is a level of autonomy and flexibility in school-level management. The ongoing, dynamic national reform movement currently involves all provinces which make frequent adjustments responding to feedback from local areas. The main responsibilities of national, provincial, municipal, county, and township levels are distinguished as follows.

The *central government* retains authority for creating basic laws and policies, sets development direction, prepares medium and long-term national plans, supervises implementation, provides coordination of regional programs; conducts national research and development; monitors education outcomes, disseminates successful experiences to lower levels; promotes equity in education services; designs national curriculum; and sets national education standards (e.g., teacher qualifications, length of basic education, university entrance requirements).

The *provincial governments* implement all national laws, policies, and mandates in education. For the purpose of making adaptations to local settings, a provincial government may establish any education policies that are consistent with national policies. Examples are curriculum modifications and choice, and even development of textbooks. Provincial governments are held accountable for meeting education finance goals agreed upon in contracts between provincial and lower level governments.

The *township and village levels* are involved in financing school construction and meeting other capital expenses. The townships in a limited sense now make policy by making decisions about allocation of funds directly to schools. Townships and villages also share with the provinces responsibilities for monitoring performance. In this decentralization process, private schools have emerged. Local educationalists and scholars have begun to take the lead in developing more private and *minban* (people-run) education institutions. Such institutions are operated and financed by local communities, social organizations, and individuals who cater to evolving market needs and people's pressing demand for better education.

At the *school level,* principals manage relationships with the community, participate with school staff in the development of teaching materials, and supervise teachers. An important function of principals is the mobilization and utilization of community resources in developing flexible strategies to attain higher school quality.

The policy for all provinces in the PRC has emphasized central leadership, regional responsibility, and divided (by level) management. Much of the new policy, or national experiment, appears to be working remarkably well. However, the PRC has experienced serious problems of inequity across and within provinces during devolution. There appears frequently to be a trade-off between equity in education opportunities and the flexibility, adaptiveness, and innovation achieved through decentralization (Box 3). Additionally, many technical planning difficulties constrain effective decentralized operations.

The range in available local resources in the PRC has led to a range in the amount of capital construction, level of teachers' salaries, and quality of school facilities. Generally, areas with higher incomes and more financial resources provide better education services than the poorer areas. The distinction can be enormous. For example, in 1985 the ratio of the per capita education expenditures in the eastern, central, and western parts of the PRC was 1:0.80:0.71, and in 1995 the ratio was 1:0.62:0.54 (Zhou 1997). The extent to which such disparities have led to differences in education output is unclear.

The PRC has placed heavy demand on regional human resource planning, at times distinguishing between coastal and interior areas. The coastal areas, which are comparatively rich in technical and scientific personnel and advanced education facilities, have encouraged the development of both small town enterprises and larger export-oriented industries. These efforts are seen as very significant to total national output. Education reform at all levels is expected to contribute, particularly in terms of supply of human resources, to these national economic development programs.

The unprecedented growth of an export-oriented economy has led to urgent problems in education. One problem concerns demand for skills produced by basic education. Another question is how regional higher education institutions can strengthen the training of complex talents needed for further development of the export-oriented economy and thus help increase the PRC's competitiveness among the international market economies.

Box 3: Inequities Resulting from Decentralization – The PRC

As pointed out by Cheng (1994, 62), decentralization in the PRC has facilitated local initiatives and mobilized local resources. Much of the achievement in the country's basic education during the past decade is attributable to the introduction of decentralization. However, Cheng observes (p.62), "China is not immune from the usual disease – regional disparity – which is brought about by decentralization."

For poor communities, decentralization has meant a perpetuation of financial shortage. "To them," Cheng remarks, "if schools are to survive, money has to come from elsewhere, presumably from the 'state.' To these places, the central government would regain its legitimacy only if it could resume its financial responsibility in education." The disparity is not only a matter of economics. It reflects a tug-of-war between the ideology of the planned economy on the one hand, and the ideology of the market economy on the other.

The challenge to policymakers, thus, is the creation of a completely new model of education governance, with all the necessary accompaniments of individual skills, institutional capacities and resources. The challenge to planners and administrators is to provide useful information to policymakers and to make the new model particularly responsive to local and regional evolving economic demands.

The India Case

The scope of constitutional, legal, and administrative changes made possible through comprehensive education decentralization policies is well illustrated by the case of India. As in many Asian countries the policy making, planning, and administration of schools in India is a complex process carried out through a number of institutions at various levels. With many widely dispersed schools, poor vertical and horizontal communication, and limited capabilities in monitoring and evaluation, achieving effective management is difficult. Over the years there have been many efforts at partly decentralizing decisions to the district level. These have met with limited success.

In 1992, India laid the foundation for a significantly different pattern of education governance by amending its national constitution. This action was seen as important both symbolically and substantively. The 73rd constitutional amendment authorized states to establish a three-tiered (village, block, and district) governance structure of locally elected bodies – the "Panchayati Raj" institutions – and to transfer to these bodies certain authorities from state government agencies. Primary education was one of the most important areas to come under the Panchayati Raj institutions (Box 4).

These changes brought new roles and new stakeholders at each political

Box 4: The Panchayati Raj Initiative – India

Jain and Hochgesang (1995) are among analysts of India's Panchayati Raj initiative. They explain that:

As a part of the long process of evaluation of institutional framework for the development of rural areas, the system of Panchayati Raj assumed impor-tance. Though the concept of democratic decentralization was to bring in the Gandhian concept of Grama Swaraj, it could not, however, be realized as it was generally affected by political and administrative factors. With the introduction of the Seventy-Third Constitutional Amendment, a new initiative for strengthening the system of Panchayati Raj was taken. For the first time adequate representation for scheduled castes, scheduled tribes, and women was provided at all levels. Five-year fixed tenure, regular elections, financial allocations, finance commissions, assignment of defined functions from planning to execution of schemes for economic development have become the major achievements of the new legislation. In spite of the fact that many questions remained regarding the functions and finances, the constitutional status accorded to the Panchayati Raj bodies will undoubtedly make them vibrant institutions for rural development.

Table 15: Responsibility of Panchayati Raj Institutions for Primary Education, Various Three-Tier Indian States, 1995

State	Zilla parishad (District)	Samiti panchayat (Taluka or block)	Gran panchayat (Village)
Andhra Pradesh		Manage elementary and higher elementary schools.	
Gujarat	Primary education: recruit primary school teachers; construct school buildings.	Establish primary school; primary education.	Primary schools.
Karnataka	Establish and maintain ashram schools; promote primary education.	Promote primary education; construct, repair and maintain schools.	Promote public awareness and participation in primary schools; ensure enrollment and attendance in primary schools.
Madhya Pradesh		Establish primary school buildings.	Inspect schools; construct and maintain primary schools; distribute free textbooks and uniforms; manage scholarships for scheduled caste/scheduled tribe primary-school children; organize nonformal education.
Maharashtra	Establish, maintain, inspect and repair primary schools; provide teaching aids to primary schools.	Primary education.	Promote education.
Rajasthan	Ensure proper functioning of primary schools.	Promote primary education.	Supervise primary schools; transfer, post, and disburse salary of primary schoolteachers.
Uttar Pradesh	Construct and maintain primary schools.	Establish and maintain primary schools.	Establish primary schools.
West Bengal	Construct primary schools in flood-affected areas; supervise primary schools.	Promote primary education.	Construct primary schools in flood-affected areas; Distribute textbooks.

Source: Jain and Hochgesang 1995.

and administrative level. The center, through the Ministry of Human Resource Development and the Department of Education, traditionally has been deeply involved in policy making, national-level planning, finance, and technical support. Under the reforms many of these functions will continue. Additionally, the central leadership in technical support to the districts is expected to increase at least for a time, and thus increase – not decrease – the challenges for the central education authorities. Generally, the changes represent a movement toward defining the role of the state as setting standards and evaluating performance. Modifications in roles include: development of a monitoring system; changing focus of research to include issues of primary education, particularly measurement of learning achievement; strengthening capacity of states to use data; and providing instructional support.

At the state level (Table 15), state ministries of education are supported by state departments and directorates or secretariats of education, all of which are accountable to the chief minister of state. At the district level – historically an important unit of administration and management but changing under the Panchayati Raj legislation – a district education officer and staff are responsible to the state department.

At the district, block, and village levels, reforms will transfer significant resources and responsibilities to Panchayati Raj institutions, including appointing and transferring teachers, allocating funds to schools, generating resources through fees and donations, and academic supervision.

At the school level, principals have been largely expected to perform a number of routine administrative tasks including drawing up timetables, establishing standards for student promotion, assigning teachers to classes, determining expenditures on instructional aids, and raising extra funds for the school. Under the reform, principals are expected to assume more responsibility in fostering a positive teaching and learning environment and assist the community in local planning.

Since the 1992 constitutional amendments, substantial changes have begun as Panchayati Raj institutions at the district, subdistrict, and village levels have become fully operational. The intent of the new framework is to lead to broad-based community support for primary education, school-level responsibility for effective instruction, and a system of professional support from higher administrative levels to lower levels.

The depth of these changes varies from state to state. But if fully implemented, the reforms will require the building of new institutional capacity, new management systems, and new individual skills. Systems of communication and coordination, particularly between district and state and between district, block, and village, need to be developed to support changing roles in policy and planning as well as resource allocation. The district as the emerging level responsible for much planning requires more sophisticated technical knowledge, monitoring and evaluation skills, and a supporting information system. At the village level, new education committees have been formed with authority for allocating resources to improve school efficiency and quality. Head teachers and community members need to become informed in their new roles in supporting teaching and learning, and in assessing school-level quality.

Achievements, Risks, and Problems

Financial, administrative, political, and education arguments can be advanced in favor of decentralization of education administration. Expected benefits include improvements in (i) education quality by encouraging decisions on management and teaching to be made by personnel closest to the school and classroom, and (ii) efficiency by freeing local education officials from layers of bureaucracy. Decentralization is also frequently seen by central ministries as a way to develop new sources for financing.

Although decentralization in various forms has a long history in some Asian countries, evaluating its progress is difficult. Several governments claim successes in implementing policies of decentralization, including PRC, India, and Thailand, and both successes and failures have been reported internationally (Bray 1999). There are also examples of communities that, without mandates from the center, participated in improving their schools. The record would seem to show, however, that central actors increasingly are willing to test new policy ideas locally, seek input from stakeholders, and include persons with field knowledge on national commissions.

Although evidence from formal evaluation is often lacking, policymakers and planners in many countries now have had the opportunity to reflect on their considerable experience in the implementation of decentralized programs. The frequently mentioned problems and constraints include:

- local authorities increase administrative activities, but control remains in the center;
- the gap in education opportunity is widened between students in wealthy and poor areas;
- central government reduces its fiscal support to local areas;
- funds collected locally are not used locally;
- the community focuses on issues of narrow self-interest;
- power over decisions becomes concentrated in local elites;
- participation is viewed as too time consuming;
- the desired level of openness and collaboration in decision making cannot be obtained;
- school administrators and teachers resist outside participation;
- local analysis of problems and supported changes may threaten the political order; and
- deciding how much participation in planning is appropriate may be very controversial.

Successful decentralized programs of education often depend on the capabilities of local government. With reference to the Pacific DMCs (Group 7), but with wider relevance, the Papua New Guinea Study for ADB (1997) notes that:

> Effective local government, which has the potential to coordinate community development and local services and infrastructure, is particularly important in countries comprising many scattered islands, yet it is noticeably weak, even dysfunctional, in most Pacific DMCs. In Western Samoa, rural water supply schemes that have been most successful are the ones in which local reluctance to participate in "self-help" schemes forced government to manage them. In many provinces in Papua New Guinea, primary health and education services run by communities

assisted by provincial governments are so poorly administered that they are in a situation of near collapse.

The study continues:

> Many donors retain faith in the idea that the inefficiency of the state apparatus can be compensated for by designing community-managed, participatory development projects, and that more effective development processes might be achieved by working directly with communities. Unfortunately, there is little evidence to show that community-managed development projects are more efficacious than those managed by the state.

Not surprisingly, new expectations for local planning and participation in education decisions may involve uncertainties, obstacles, and risks. Central bureaucracies accustomed to being the only policy and planning actors now must share responsibilities. With shifts in some functions to the district and village levels, e.g., the flow of central moneys directly to districts, stakeholders at the provincial level may lose valued control. In addition to the new policies, laws, and institutions required for a new decision-making approach, an extended period of time may be required before partnerships between levels of government can become effective (see Box 5).

Decentralization may only mean transfer of autocratic behavior to local institutions. On the other hand, local governments and communities may become highly dissatisfied if only administrative functions are delegated and neither resources nor decision-making power are transferred. At the heart of the reform process is the decentralization of powers and responsibilities from the national and provincial levels toward the district and local government

Box 5: Mobilizing Local Participation – Pakistan

The assumption of policymakers in Pakistan was that effective involvement, participation, and mobilization of communities would be effective for the promotion of basic education and improvement in quality. Unfortunately, communities are not well organized and motivated. Although a few steps in this direction have been taken by constituting village education committees, school management committees, and parent-teacher associations, their roles are not clearly defined and their linkage with the education functionaries has not been properly established.

Mahmood (1997) points out that:

There is a need to sensitize the population at large, prepare them and make them responsible for eventual take over of the local-level institutions. For this purpose empowering the District and Tehsil-level functionaries of the Education Department need to be activated to promote community mobilization and make use of their powers to give local support to communities in administrative and financial matters.

levels. Unfortunately, the issue of who is responsible for what is not often clearly understood. Further, any attempt at evaluation of the success of decentralization must raise the question: Valued by whom? Do, for example, central and provincial policymakers and planners have the same evaluation criteria as parents and teachers?

Planning and Sustaining Decentralized Education Changes

Article 7 of the 1990 World Declaration on Education for All observes that "new and revitalized partnerships at all levels will be necessary, partnerships among all subsectors and forms of education" (World Conference on Education for All 1990). The changing patterns of governance require new approaches to planning. The traditional, centralized planning model, reflected to varying degrees in the popular five-year national plans and found in most DMCs, attempts to set targets based on given or assumed priorities, translate targets into a set of inputs with associated costs, allocate responsibilities for implementation, and, perhaps, develop detailed implementation procedures. The basic assumptions of this approach include:

- general targets can be translated into specific education inputs;
- accurate data can be acquired on size, number, and costs of inputs; and
- implementation is a rather straightforward process of administrative decisions.

Experience suggests that this model is seriously flawed, as indicated by the poor record in attaining the targets of national plans.

Two fundamental assumptions of the typical centralized model are that planning is an essentially linear process, and that a discrete set of identifiable inputs will result in the desired education outputs and outcomes. This planning approach has a poor record under centralized structures, and has even less validity as decentralization proceeds. Policies of decentralization, as they develop beyond deconcentration, involve a range of local stakeholders in a process of developing and assessing ways to improve education and acquire supporting resources (Box 6). Interaction and dialogue, often in face-to-face groups, suggest a more open-ended, inquiry-oriented model of planning. Central-local partnerships, if transparent and collaborative, rely on communication and consensus, not merely political power. A new model of planning and decision making thus emerges: initial targets are temporary benchmarks of only heuristic value; expert knowledge from the outside becomes only one input to decision; information and communication among stakeholders keep the planning process moving; and education practice, as well as education research, illuminates major decisions.

The concept of central-local partnership can be controversial (Bray 2000). Partnership may be an association of individuals or groups with very different perspectives and beliefs. This relationship usually operationally involves a combination of teamwork, conflict resolution, and community collaboration.[4] Thus, success of partnerships in planning, implementation, and sustaining reform depends on the newly formed group's expectations of its members, the ability of individuals to learn from each other, and the recognition that rewards basically go to all members of the group. Collaboration may therefore include debate, argument, negotiation, discussion, and compromise. Planning and implementation of decentralization of education governance may require skills and understanding not often prominent in traditions of centralized planning.

Sustainable decentralization requires the development of new skills and insights among individuals, and additional capacity among institutions to manage education change. Required planning and actions include:

- creation of demand for improvement (given the limitations of supply-driven assistance);
- creation of reliance on local resources;
- participation and sharing of information;
- division of tasks among stakeholders;
- identification of stakeholders;
- diagnosis of community needs and types of support;
- identification of relevant existing local organizations;
- formulation of methodology for mobilization of the community;
- development of technology for planning, implementation, and moni-toring; and
- capacity building and long-term commitment.

Sustainability depends on adequately answering the basic question: What decision-making authority is best allocated to each administrative level? And the correlative question: Which education activities are best carried out at which level? The answers can be tested only through experience and may vary from country to country and by local context. Moreover, there are further questions: Best for whom? Where are the economies of scale? What are the comparative advantages of different management options?

At the school level, sustainability requires at least three conditions: shared goals regarding the learning objectives of the school; professional, student-focused commitment among teachers; and autonomy to allocate instructional resources flexibly. There is also an obligation to hold the school accountable to the community for outcomes in the context of national indicators. These are challenges for which many education systems are ill prepared.

---

[4] Shaeffer (1992, 280) makes the following distinction between collaboration and decentralization: *collaboration* is a consultative process at best, where the new actors share the burden with the traditional administrators of education and help improve the conditions of classroom teaching, to enhance the effectiveness and efficiency of schools, and to deliver their services, without quite becoming a "partner" in the process. *Participation* would add 'intervention' to the above definition: the ability to get involved in governance, policy, and administration; to serve as a more equal partner in planning, managing, and evaluation; and to gain power (and empowerment) through the process.

The changes in governance with decentralization of certain authorities and increased involvement of citizens in education and political decisions require increased levels of information and analytical ability. Sustainability suggests the need for learning through continued cycles of design, redesign, study, evaluation, exchange of information, action, etc. The typical monitoring is unlikely to be sufficient if it is limited to tracking the delivery of goods and expenditures of funds and if it relies only on the traditional mid-term and final program and project evaluations. Fundamentally, this process needs both a planning and evaluation process that assists the development and critique of information and communication processes that foster individual and organizational learning; and a political and administrative context in which such learning translates into monitored actions and continued inquiry.

In developing systems of decentralization, two basic questions suggest a fundamental choice: Is the central government willing to support local conditions that lead to full partnership in the planning of education and community-level ownership of significant education decisions? Or is the prime interest to foster a centrally controlled system that more effectively monitors local units?

Improving School-Community Relations

Williams (1997) compares "government-provided education" with "collaborative government-community education" (Table 16). Certainly, over the last several decades much of the remarkable growth and development of education in DMCs is attributable to "government-provided education." The changing patterns of education governance, however, responding to limitations of central management, have brought a new focus on local communities and their relationships with schools.

Most communities face a number of shared education problems, such as fees and other costs borne by parents, school-work relationships, and persistent dropouts. Such concerns, under certain conditions, may provide a common purpose and a sense of priorities, and may facilitate community dialogue on school matters. Supporting conditions include: experience of the community in participatory decision making;[5] willingness of governments to share control while continuing to provide resources; and commitment on the part of public and private organizations involved to a process of continuing learning. The latter condition implies that coping strategies or solutions to problems emerge from examination and study of local experience as well as from analysis by outside technical expertise (Shaeffer 1992).

Understanding the potential for constructive community-school relationships requires examining who the participants are, what the contributions are that the community can make to the school, and the ways in which the school

---

[5] Reimers (1997, 148) suggests that the kind of intelligence needed to address school problems at the local level is process intelligence, not intelligence about contents. What is most needed is a change in paradigm regarding how education systems change and learn from their experience, rather than a set of policy prescriptions to be implemented by schools.

can support the community (Bray 2000). Those individuals and organizations particularly significant in bringing school and community together include parents, teachers, local government, NGOs, women's groups, local enterprises, colleges and universities, government through its laws, policies, and education bureaucracy, and international organizations.

Schools, for their part, can share information, technical knowledge and facilities, and can contribute labor to community projects. Efforts in these directions can build a foundation of understanding, making community support more feasible. Communities, of course, are not of one mind, and may not place a high priority on education. Yet, given the ongoing interest or possibility of mobilization, the types of possible school support are numerous. The contributions of community involvement to schools may be grouped under three areas: support for the instructional program, supplements to school resources, and managing the schools (Table 17).

The potential risks involved in devolution of education responsibility and authority were discussed earlier. In some cases, there will be setbacks to reforms that have moved support and management of schools. Agreement on

Table 16: Models of School and Community in the Provision of Education

	Education providers		
	Traditional community-based education	*Government-provided education*	*Collaborative government-community education*
Purpose of education	Socialization into community; Survival of community.	Socialization into national culture; Political, economic development of state.	Socialization into national and local cultures; serves local and national improvement.
Nature of knowledge to be acquired	Transmission of local economic skills and community norms.	Transmission of state-approved knowledge.	Negotiable; usually state-approved knowledge adapted to local needs.
Emphasis	On community.	On individual and state.	On individual as member of both community and state.
Vision of community's role	All-encompassing.	Passive recipient; Potentially disruptive of government's project.	Negotiable; ranging from community as focal point of development effort to community as important arm of the government.
Role of government	None to the extent that government does not interfere.	Assumes complete responsibility for provision of education.	Negotiable; ranging from source of support for education defined by community to virtually complete control.

Source: Williams 1997, 57.

resource allocation to provincial and local levels has had ill effects. Even communities capable of organizing themselves successfully to participate in addressing the problems do not necessarily agree on the types of solution. And building and implementing strategic plans and plans of action may require unavailable technical skills. However, with the involvement of major stakeholders, capacity to acquire necessary resources, and persistent leadership, the benefits can be long lasting not only in education but also in the strengthening of other sectors.

Table 17: How Involvement of the Community Can Improve Education

Area of education	Type of community involvement
Provide support for instructional program	• Cultivate an environment supportive of school program • Improve enrollment, retention, attendance • Monitor study at home • Ensure all students have adequate study space • Identify and help students with problems • Help students with family emergencies • Boost morale of school staff • Provide assistant or regular teachers • Provide instruction in specific areas (where teachers lack expertise) • Pass on community knowledge • Provide apprenticeships/work opportunities
Supplement school resources	• Donate land for school • Donate labor/materials to build/help build school building • Repair/maintain facilities • Donate equipment, learning aids (e.g., books, teaching materials) • Raise money for school
Provide support for school management	• Ensure greater likelihood for successful implementation of school programs • Foster responsibility among parents for children's learning • Provide greater material support • Provide manpower to reduce burden on school staff • Supply expertise • Assist in fund-raising, provide moral support and general advice • Provide new ideas, serve troubleshooting functions • Serve on advisory/management committees • Assume joint responsibility (with school) for planning, managing, evaluating local school programs • Come to assume, over time, major responsibility for local education, formal and informal, with government support and technical assistance • Take over most of the management functions of the school, with minimal government assistance

Source: Williams 1997, 63.

Emerging Education Trends and Strategies

Earlier sections of this booklet analyzed the behavior of education systems within the context of economic, demographic, and social change. This section turns to education trends and strategies. It begins with issues of governance before turning to issues of quality. It also stresses the need for improved indicators and information.

Education Governance and Management

One type of education reform that cuts across all county groupings and is found in most, but not all, DMCs is the movement toward some form of education decentralization. Although the motivation and expectations for the reform vary across countries, the locus of education action is moving away from the center "downward." These changes appear to invalidate further exclusive reliance on traditional centralized planning as a mechanism for developing and maintaining effective education systems. The role of the state in DMCs, especially in terms of responsibility for the governance, planning, and management of education, is changing rapidly and is being dynamically redefined. Adjustments are being made in assignment of responsibilities in areas such as:

- planning (strategic planning and budgeting, school-level use of resources);
- education finance (financing of current and capital expenditures);
- curriculum (development, design and content, production and distribution of teaching materials);
- teachers (recruitment, qualifications, training, salaries);
- supervision (supervision of academic performance in school, assistance in improving performance);
- facilities (school construction and maintenance); and
- evaluation (testing of student achievement, dissemination of results).

The merits and limitations of decentralization of education responsibilities will be the foci of continuing national discussion and debates. A related debate, and subject to change as new insights emerge from experience, concerns assignment of responsibilities, and decision-making authority at different administrative levels.

Policy 1. Strengthening of Institutional Infrastructure in the Center

Such strengthening is needed generally to promote efficiency and transparency in decision making and, more specifically, because new functions and responsibilities are being transferred from central governments as education policy and planning are decentralized.

> *Strategies:*
> - *Articulation and communication of the national vision and strategies for the reform to personnel at all levels in the education sector, other government sectors, and to the public.* National ministries associated with education, because of their understanding of the purpose, content, and management implications, are in the best position to mobilize support from other government agencies, inform the public, and develop opportunities for citizen input. If the full support of local communities is sought, then the national vision should demonstrate a respect for the potential of communities as partners.
> - *Development of supporting laws, policies, and guidelines, and provision of strategic and implementation plans for ongoing technical assistance to local management levels.* An initial action in the center could be the restructuring and streamlining of central education offices to eliminate overlapping of functions, to reconfigure directorates and subdirectorates, and, as necessary, to retrain personnel. Second, the necessary technical skills for planning and managing for the new responsibilities may be in short supply at the provincial and district levels. Large-scale, monitored training and continuous technical assistance will likely be needed. Distribution of excess skilled staff from the central offices to provincial and district levels may help overcome human resource shortages. Since reforms and financing go together, local governments are likely to need central assistance in generating resources and may need authority to raise revenues. Planning for resource provision may need to be differentiated by variations in the resource-generating capacities of local governments.
> - *Further development of research and development, monitoring, and evaluation functions in the center.* As the decentralization process evolves, center institutions will move from roles that emphasize policies, plans, and control-oriented administration toward roles that focus on decision-oriented research, setting new standards, creating the conditions, and providing resources for developing demonstration and experimental programs. Generating and applying knowledge on the behavior of the education systems is a requisite for successful management of programmatic and institutional changes.

Policy 2. Improving Education Planning and Policy Capabilities of Provincial and District Institutions

Provisional and district leadership in some areas of planning and management are evolving. The difficulty and complexity of decision making and management are not diminished by moving the locus of education decisions downward. New problems emerge related to resource generation and allocation, personnel (which may include teachers and administrators) selection and placement, and evaluation of schooling. In planning and organizing education change, provincial and local education authorities may need to cope with a social and political environment that includes an entrenched structure of political power, competing interests among stakeholders, and patterns of social divisions that inhibit consensus-based decision making. A well-planned implementation process can be expected to include opportunities for concurrent staff development and a piloting phase of the reforms.

Strategies:
- *Policies and regulations developed to specify policy and planning authority established at the province and district levels.* Devolution of education responsibilities and authority moves vertically and sometimes horizontally. These processes are well under way in several DMCs, and cases of authority transfers to provincial and district levels currently can be found in various countries, including PRC, India, and Pakistan.
- *Plans and programs for development of training in a range of new individual skills and institutional capacities to assess education needs, monitor progress, and provide supervision.* Given that technical skills, monitoring systems, sets of indicators, and information systems do not guarantee a successful process of planning and sustaining of effective education programs, also needed may be conditions to create and maintain dialogue involving local stakeholders and participants. Absence of dialogue among stakeholders rather than the lack of resources may be the major inhibiting factor. A more participatory planning process with involvement of stakeholders is no guarantee either of higher-quality schooling nor of expanded education opportunities. However, if centralization amounts only to the application of new control mechanisms of the central government, then parents and communities remain powerless and potentially apathetic to acceptance of additional responsibilities. Increasingly in those countries where local forms of education responsibility are sustained, there will be a need for strengthening district and community capacity for quality control, monitoring, and evaluation. In this process a number of organizations, e.g., United Nations Children's Fund (UNICEF), UNESCO, and international and national NGOs with experience of local governments and community organizations, can play an important role. Also worthy of consideration are partnerships with universities and other research and training bodies.

- *Development of communication and information networks across provinces, districts, and schools.* Some of the leadership activities at the central level, e.g., public dialogue, coordinating critical support groups and organizations, are replicated at the provincial level. And, with provincial monitoring, the district in some DMCs is evolving into a key level for planning and facilitating collaboration across schools, communities, and school clusters.

Policy 3. Restructuring School-Level Management

Some of the planning and most of the action of school improvement takes place at the school and community levels. Decentralization places additional expectations on school management at the site and community levels. Planning and sustaining changes in classrooms and schools depends on the ability to develop collaborative relations with the community; monitor school quality and efficiency; generate, understand, and utilize information on interventions in progress; and to respond to the emergence of new priorities. Principals and citizens' committees may need to (i) promote access and equity by adjusting costs to ability to pay through modification of fee requirements, development of student loan programs, reduction of opportunity costs by incorporating income-generating activities into the curriculum; (ii) adapt the quality and relevance of the curriculum by including local materials, providing initial instruction in the child's home language, and developing self-instructional and modular materials; and (iii) develop school programs to respond to community problems – by sharing school resources, information, ideas, and labor.

A central question to be addressed by local planners and managers is how parents and communities can be helped increase capabilities to plan and assess education choices, mobilize, and monitor options. This question suggests actions for which school principals, teachers, and parents typically are inexperienced, have few support resources, and have too little information to make informed decisions (Chapman 2002).

Strategies:
- *Retraining of principals in new requirements for managing schools or districts, including financial management, instructional supervision, and community liaison.* A basic objective is to assist the principals, teachers, and other school staff to be more independent and more creative in improving schools as places of learning.
- *Development of local systems for monitoring education quality, including needs assessment technologies, use of indicators, and development of data analysis capabilities.* Local strategic planning will be needed to analyze local conditions, set objectives, and mobilize community efforts. Implementation of instructional, management, and assessment procedures requires action plans.

Policy 4. Regional Research and Training Role for ADB

It is important that ADB recognize that the process and actors in policy making, planning and, to a degree, education evaluation are changing, even though the extent and results of change are not easily predictable. The need to determine the role of ADB as a partner in this reform should be an ADB priority. The importance of this partnership is based on the assumption that a focus on support for country, regional, and local policy reforms through assistance in planning, evaluation, management, and institutional capacity building can potentially influence the quality, efficiency, equity, and relevance of all subsectors of the education systems. ADB's response to and involvement in this trend may include encouragement and assistance in providing a research and information base, and helping to build institutional capacity for planning, managing, and evaluating local education programs. Central to this task will be assessment of training needs and the technical and professional upgrading of education personnel at all levels of management.

Strategies:
- *Exploration of the potential for cross-country research and training related to evolving patterns of decentralization.* ADB, with its regional concerns and expertise, may consider encouraging a regional, cross-country dialogue and a program of supporting research to synthesize the insight being acquired from the implementation of evolving patterns of decentralization. One focus on research and training could be on the impact of decentralization on local communities with the purpose of empowering local groups to cope with the new problems and opportunities. If requested, ADB, in collaboration with DMCs and other international agencies, could assist in organizing such research and training and become a world center for Asian research on implementation of new modes of education governance.

Developing and Sustaining High-Quality, Equitable, and Adequately Financed Education Systems

Education systems are made up of interdependent levels and institutions. Policies and investments focusing on only one education level to the exclusion of others may create distortions (Heyneman 1997). An example from the past would be the strong priority given by some countries to higher education at the expense of other levels. Similarly, investment in basic education should be viewed as a necessary but insufficient condition for the development of education systems. The interdependence of levels and programs of the system is readily demonstrated in the necessity for articulation of curriculum and examinations between system levels. Indeed, the quality and efficiency of each successive level is strongly influenced by those characteristics in preceding levels. It is further shown, because the system is staffed by its own products, that the quality of higher education affects teaching and administration throughout the system. In planning their futures, DMCs should seek not only high-quality basic education, but also high-quality secondary and tertiary education.

Policy 1. Developing Effective Basic Education

Traditional arguments for giving priority to basic education include:

- the rate of return on investments in basic education, particularly in less developed countries, is higher than for secondary or tertiary education;
- basic schooling, again particularly in less developed countries, has a high, independent impact on the academic achievement of children; and
- at least prior to the latter stages of universalization, basic education may contribute to social mobility.

Thus, there appear to be both economic and social equity reasons to justify priority. If it may be assumed that expenditure per student has a direct relationship with quality, then the quality gap between high- and low-income countries is increasing. Appropriately, improving education quality is an expressed goal in all DMCs. Education quality in terms of level and utility of what pupils learn in schools is demonstrably poor in most low- and middle-income countries.

There remain populations of significant size in several countries and in the poorer areas of most DMCs without access to basic education in any form. Some of these populations have initially enrolled for a brief period in school, and others have never attended school. The disadvantages of the absence of education last a lifetime for members of this group. This condition also lessens the overall quality of society and most particularly creates a vicious cycle of fewer employment opportunities, less income, and fewer chances for advancement in the job. It also creates families less able to afford education for their children. The problems of equity involve not only girls but also the rural and urban poor, linguistic and ethnic minorities, and populations in remote areas. This situation is particularly acute, for example, in Bhutan, PRC, India, Nepal, and Pakistan, and in certain island populations in Indonesia and the Philippines. Provision of increased education opportunities to this population will be relatively costly, and will test the seriousness of commitment to equity of both governments and international agencies. If the concept of equity is extended to include not only access to schooling but also equitable outcomes in terms of access to resources, participation, leadership, and reward in society, then discriminatory practices are found in every country. Increased education opportunities are but one, and perhaps the easiest, of several necessary ameliorating policies.

Priorities and Strategies for Basic Education

- *A sector or subsector analysis of the requisite everyday and work skills most needed by citizens, and the capability of schools to provide such skills.* The issue for any given country becomes: What kind of basic education? Leaving aside the question of the validity of the research underlying the justification for investment, emerging economic and workplace conditions suggest the need for a redefinition of basic education. For countries that are primarily agricultural and utilize a low level of technology, the meaning of basic education may be different from those more technologically advanced. For countries moving rapidly into industrialization and mechanized agriculture, a different, more complex – although still high-priority – basic education will be needed. Priority interventions should focus on such areas as teachers and teaching, teacher motivation, curriculum, school management, community support, and alternative delivery systems.

- *Development and implementation of a national instructional development strategy elaborated through input by local administrators and teachers.* Such a strategy or policy may be crucial for the planning of the quality aspect of basic education, and should respond to new skill and knowledge requirements of economic productivity and to continuing or new social and familial objectives. The strategy should be informed by international and national research on effective schooling to help determine a core set of interventions worthy of evaluation within local contexts. Included in such a policy could be strategies related to the use of instructional time; instructional materials and instructional style; strategies for coping with individual differences; minimum teacher standards; guidelines and support for principals; and the development of school-level indicators to measure multidimensional learnings, not merely academic achievement. The learning implications of trade-offs between inputs, e.g., poorly paid teachers with small classes versus adequately paid teachers with larger classes, should be explored.

- *Special programs of financial and instructional support for the poor.* Problems of access, equity, quality, and finance tend to be particularly severe among the poor and in remote areas. Children are unable to attend school, or drop out of school, for a wide variety of reasons. Although basic education may be defined differently by country, it is assumed to include all children, if feasible for a country's resources. International experience provides lessons on a broad array of scholarships and other financial assistance schemes targeted at the support of poor children. Special instructional support may need to include some form of distance education to reach peripheral populations.

- *Special scholarships and other assistance for girls from poor families.* Access percentages are not an adequate measure of gender equity. Education authorities have a responsibility to work with other govern-

ment agencies to create the circumstances and conditions for gender parity in educational and social opportunities.
- *Education opportunities for the physically and learning impaired.* With encouragement from the center, the education authorities may take leadership in creating integrated programs in nutrition, health, and special education for this population.
- *Experimentation with new delivery systems, e.g., multigrade class-rooms, distance teaching, low-cost technologies.* Resources may not be the critical constraint in school improvement. Allocation of additional funds does not necessarily lead to more effective schools. Education systems vary greatly in the learning gains acquired from similar levels of investments. Initiation of programs implemented in highly industri-alized countries may prove too costly for less developed countries.

Policy 2. Developing Effective Secondary Education

Allocation of funds between levels of education will be a persistent issue. However, policies and programs for improvements in secondary education and higher education development cannot wait until objectives of high-quality basic education are fully achieved, since the latter are dependent on the former. Moreover, rapid expansion of basic education accompanied by an influx of enrollments into secondary education creates new problems for secondary and higher education. Risks of unemployment or low income may no longer be confined to early school-leavers, and may include those with secondary and higher education certification without adequate basic skills. Reports from DMCs indicate a growing concern with the current effectiveness of secondary education. Growth is taxing the adequacy of public sector funding. Decision makers may face a dilemma of allocation of resources to existing higher-quality secondary schools or extending funding to create more delivery options and expanding the supply of schools in rural areas. The weak link of secondary education to employment has encouraged the search for workable linkages with industry and the reduction of traditional distinctions between education and training.

A distinction needs to be made between countries that have largely achieved universal primary and basic education (Groups 2, 6, and several countries in Group 3) and those that have not (Groups 4 and 5). The former are likely to give priority to the demand for upper secondary and higher education for the growing population of youth completing basic education.

Priorities and Strategies for Secondary Education
- *Planning and assessment of secondary education in terms of its contribution to the cohesive structure of the system.* Entrance and exit standards may need to be created in keeping with national and local preferences and congruent with the initial and tertiary levels of edu-cation.
- *Initial planning for extension of basic education through junior secon-dary schools.* Especially for countries in which universalization has

not been attained, the priority may be to achieve high-quality primary education. Nevertheless, the planning for the extension of basic education into eight or nine years requires a considerable lead time to avoid crises in quality of staff.

- *Further development of the quality and relevance of secondary education in terms of evolving economic conditions.* This strategy would especially apply to those countries undergoing rapid industrialization, and those in transition to market-driven economic systems. As enrollments expand, several pathways should be developed for secondary education and training, while protecting the transferability across programs. A variety of delivery modes – public and private, formal and nonformal, general and specialized – will be needed to meet the range of demands for secondary education, testing the creativity and capabilities for coordination of central and local governments. Many of these options will necessarily include academic senior secondary schools, general types of vocational education, existing vocational and technical schools and training centers, highly specialized vocational secondary education, apprenticeships, a wide variety of school-enterprise arrangements, and new combinations of general and work-related programs. The challenge to policymakers is to achieve diversification of programs within acceptable levels of cost effectiveness.

    Since youth violence and delinquency are on the rise in several DMCs, particularly in urban centers, secondary schools should participate in and perhaps take the leadership of national youth policies. The opportunity to volunteer service and meet community obligations may add to the personal development of youth and encourage their respect for schooling.

- *If necessary, reservation of a number of school places for girls, and information on the number of such places should be widely disseminated.* If conditions so require, single-sex schools should be created. The long-term goal is to equalize access and graduation rates for males and females at all three levels of education.

Policy 3. Developing Effective Tertiary Education

The expansion of the system has already reached higher education in the economically more advanced countries in East and Southeast Asia. Among the three levels of education, from 1990 through 2010 higher education will show the greatest growth. As higher education ceases to be a privilege for a small elite, the market returns from diplomas and other certification will be reduced. A major planning, management, and political question emerges: Who coordinates growth and change in this interdependent system to ensure that there is articulation between levels and the whole system is of acceptable quality? Although various professional organizations may monitor components of the education sector, much of this task will reside with central or provincial agencies.

Priorities and Strategies for Tertiary Education
*   *Development of responsiveness of tertiary education to other parts of the system in terms of standards, admission criteria, and curriculum.* Easy transfers across programs and inter-institutional transfers and exchanges should be facilitated. A policy framework may be needed that encourages autonomy by providers, responds to demand, and supports continuing development of teaching and administrative staff. Multiple channels of funding should be utilized. However, governments must decide where public responsibility ends and where private responsibility begins. The funding sources and their management may be different for tertiary education than for other levels. Like other levels, however, tertiary education has a responsibility to help develop public willingness to make education investments. Women's access and treatment in higher education continue to be a special concern. Enrollment projections demonstrate a significant continuing gap into the 21st century in tertiary education between males and females. In addition to exploration of the feasibility of a variety of scholarship schemes, places set aside for women may be needed.

Developing Better Indicators and Information

The devolution of education dialogue and decisions, and the emergence of local strategic education planning, require that new kinds of data, information, and indicators be made available and analyzed at provincial, local, and school levels. Local, national, and cross-national data for informed decisions are commonly not available in many DMCs. This is true at all levels of education policy making, planning, and evaluation from the central education bureaucracy to the school.

The current information systems in DMCs, even if well developed, typically have been designed primarily to support centralized education policy making, planning, and administration. Accordingly, information on schooling moves vertically from school to district to province, then finally to the central level. As planning and implementation of education reform gradually shift to the lower levels of the education bureaucracy, and as new local institutions and networks emerge, information is needed for decision making at these levels. Some of the information needed may already be collected at the school level. In the past, however, little analysis has taken place at this level.

The commonality among education reforms suggests that regionally designed indicators would facilitate cross-country dialogue and research. The preparation of, and exploratory use of, well-developed education indicators could be a valuable continuing training experience for policymakers, planners and researchers.

Policy 1. Strengthening the Policy Relevance of a Regional System of Education Indicators

Better education indicators can help policymakers, administrators, and citizens to monitor national education changes and facilitate cross-country com- parisons. When available, carefully constructed indicators allow countries to see themselves in light of performances of other countries. Of equal importance, the local, national, and regional information generated by indicators can inform policy and program dialogue. The monitoring and evaluation of education at all levels is crucial in effective system development, and requires a theoretically grounded and operationally viable indicator system. One of the best sets of education indicators is being developed by the Organisation for Economic Co-operation and Development (OECD). These indicators, and the dialogue that led to their development and use, go well beyond current practice in most Asian DMCs, and provide information on crucial aspects in education policy (OECD 1997).

Strategies:
- *Development over time of (i) a regional education indicator system, (ii) new information collection and processing capacities at the provin- cial and district levels, and (iii) on-site assessment and monitoring capabilities at the school level.* Regional collaboration with ADB as one partner could help develop a set of indicators to guide much improved country databases. It would provide important insights into the development of the sector and subsectors of education, allow better monitoring of national education changes, and facilitate cross- country comparisons. This undertaking should be a cooperative effort involving ADB, the World Bank, UNESCO and perhaps other interna- tional agencies, ministries of education, scholars of education, planning bodies, and national bureaus of statistics (see Chapman 2002). The indicator set should include attention to each major policy area, but also probe deeply into areas where other indicator sets are weak, such as the learning environment, education and work, home conditions, and student achievement.

Developing More Effective International Assistance

ADB documents describe a commitment to a sector approach. This approach includes an emphasis on capacity building, a focus on basic education, and encouragement of multiple delivery systems, including NGOs and private deliverers. ADB also claims to be increasing its focus on process, and fostering participation. Such statements suggest the direction of ADB and can be interpreted as a policy commitment to flexibility and responsiveness to the preferences of the recipient countries.

Information from the country sector studies commissioned by ADB in 1997 in eight DMCs (PRC, Indonesia, Kyrgyz Republic, Nepal, Pakistan, Papua New Guinea, Philippines, and Viet Nam) reveals the importance of many of the projects and programs supported by ADB. All eight countries, including those in which ADB has been involved for only a few years, observe that ADB has contributed to positive changes in education, particularly in poverty reduction projects and programs to increase opportunities for girls' access to schooling. Moreover, all these countries are anticipating increased ADB support in the future. At least some of the positive contributions attributed to ADB, e.g., female education in rural Nepal, have been made in areas where government programs were nonexistent or inadequate.

These country studies also conclude that there is room for significant improvement in the sensitivity of ADB operations to country priorities, and in the effectiveness of project implementation. The issues identified by these cases revolve around:

- the relationship between ADB and governments in choice of projects;
- problems of implementation;
- difficulties of sustainability; and
- the long-term impact of extensive involvement by external agencies on the credibility of the education bodies in recipient countries.

Within ADB's general policy and commitments to improving the delivery of assistance, the following sets of strategies are discussed.

Strategy 1. Improving Operational Coordination between ADB and DMC Governments

Governments have not yet fully learned how to work with international agencies, and vice versa. The government bodies established or designated as responsible for donor coordination, some of which have been created recently, have not always been effective. At times several bodies are negotiating separately with ADB, thus reducing the power of the central coordinating body. Moreover, there may be individual motivations in the form of additional income and other perquisites that influence the intracountry competition for ADB projects. As one government official told the author, "You are nobody unless you are participating in an internationally funded project." The following quotations taken from the country sector studies commissioned by ADB in 1997 are indicative of this concern:

(i)   *Nepal.* "Although the Ministry of Education is supposed to take up the role of coordination of donor contributions, there is no mechanism and process that ensure that the coordination is taken up effectively and efficiently" (Shakya et al. 1998, 42).

(ii) *Philippines.* "Often project proposals are seriously debated within the donor agency even before the Philippine government has fully considered their merits. The bottom line is that it is seldom the government pushing for the projects" (Manugue et al. 1997, 46).

(iii) *Papua New Guinea.* "Donor funding in education could be made more effective if policy priorities and needs of the department are defined more clearly. In this way, any donor funded initiative can be driven by the needs of government and not as a donor-driven initiative. It is beholden on the recipient to put all aid to productive use in its development efforts" (Papua New Guinea 1997, 62).

(iv) *PRC.* "If a project is implemented to solve key issues and weak links in education in China, international organizations [should] adopt the assistance strategy suited to China's actual conditions and if assistance effectiveness is relevant to education, the efficiency will be high. The coordination and active support among the relevant government departments is a basic guarantee for success in the project" (Zhou 1997, 3-4).

(v)   *Pakistan.* "Donors and the government officials, in general, agree [on priorities and strategies]." However, "greater coordination is needed at the provincial level where schools are managed and operated" (Mahmood 1997, 51-2).

(vi) *Viet Nam.* "There is a difficulty in combining objectives identified by international donors and the objectives of development of Viet Namese education" (Viet Nam 1997, 66).

Strategy 2. Monitoring Program and Project Implementation

Project implementation and sustainability apparently are ubiquitous problems with new projects and programs in all DMCs and perhaps worldwide. All the eight country studies identified weaknesses in capability to carry projects through successful implementation. The Papua New Guinea sector study (Papua New Guinea 1997, 64) pointed out that:

> Large donor projects tend to lose, in their grandness, the smaller community development and community involvement components, and result

in the alienation of the very communities and people that need and must feel involved.

The sector study from the Philippines noted (Manugue et al. 1997, paras. 2.49, 2.50) that:

> The project proposal may have been designed by the consultant with impressive technical precision; however, local capacities may not be fully prepared to implement the project. The donors [should] also [be] active in the area of technology transfer with the technical guidance and expertise that they provide.

The sector study from the PRC emphasized government involvement (Zhou 1997, 4):

> The role of the government is the essential factor. It is hard to implement the project without the government support.

Strategy 3. Improving Program and Project Sustainability

Sustainability goes well beyond usual definitions of implementation by implying a long-term continued development of the initiated education changes. Lack of sustainability of assistance projects and programs appears to be a common concern among DMCs. The Papua New Guinea sector study, for example, provided two examples of agency-supported projects that may not be sustainable once external funding ends (Papua New Guinea 1997, 64):

> The World Bank textbook printing project is behind schedule and indeed in danger of lapsing because of the government's inability to meet the cost of the recurrent component. There must be a change in donor and government thinking on this issue if progress is to be made. Without support to government recurrent counterpart funding implementation of many projects will not occur. Donors currently show little enthusiasm for such a change but the impasse must be solved. Perhaps donors should move more to *sectoral investment* instead of looking at specific projects, thus allowing the financing of recurrent costs and ensuring the implementation of projects.

> The Port Moresby National High School [assisted by Japanese aid] is an example of a negative effect of donor assistance as it is a very expensive exercise that has left government with unacceptable maintenance and recurrent costs. It is an example of the monument-building approach to aid which not only leaves large recurrent costs but also raises expectations to a level way beyond the realms of reality. The argument that such projects cost government no money is not acceptable. Similar problems face government with the proposal to build a K15 million high school at Kiunga in the Western Province.

As the two cases cited above suggest, long-term program development is often constrained by the recurrent costs. Adequate recurrent budgets are crucial both in support of ongoing investments, e.g., salaries for teachers in additional schools, and to implement and sustain new investments, e.g., development of viable new training and research institutions. Thus projects and programs related to education expansion or reform may be generated by an investment budget heavily reliant on external loans without careful consideration given to future demands on recurrent budgets.

Strategy 4. Continuing Dialogue on Long-Term Dangers of Extensive ADB Assistance

Linked to the worry about sustainability is an overall concern for the potential of international assistance creating a dependency of countries on external moneys. The Pakistan sector study (Mahmood 1997) notes that:

> After the evaluation of SAP-1 [Social Action Programme] and other ADB funded projects, there is a growing concern about the sustainability of education expenditure for the enhanced education network, in particular, nondevelopment and recurring costs. The government has limited resources and budget for education and other social sectors, and it seems difficult to manage huge expansion of the education sector by the government sources alone.

The Papua New Guinea sector study observes (Papua New Guinea 1997, 64) that:

> It is becoming evident that government is becoming increasingly dependent on external donor assistance to fund the investment component of the budget. There is also evidence that an increasing proportion of recurrent costs of the development budget is now being taken up by donors.

In agreement, the Philippines sector study explains (Manugue et al. 1997, para. 2.46) that:

> One of the issues against relying on Overseas Development Assistance sources for funding is the *perception* that it fosters dependency.... Moreover, asking assistance from foreign donors offends the sensibilities of some Filipinos who believe that it builds an image of the Filipinos as mendicants.

The sector studies offer several suggestions for making international assistance more effective. In short, the country analyses conclude that the receiving country must:

- clearly identify and make available its own priorities;
- maintain a central coordinating body which enforces policies and regulations related to external assistance; and
- require more planned communication and collaboration between aid agencies.

Concerning the last of these, the country sector studies generally agree that communication among aid agencies over the past few years has improved, but argue that the level of coordination remains inadequate. The condition sought is for what the Pakistan country sector study calls a more "effective partnership" between government and ADB, and a relationship in which, in the words of the Papua New Guinea study, "the donors become partners in development reacting to government initiatives, not the other way around."

Conclusion

The Asian and Pacific region is a highly diverse and rapidly changing region, exhibiting great variation across and within ADB's DMCs in population, size, economic growth, and patterns of culture. However, some commonalties can be identified in the challenges faced as education becomes recognized as a central concern in attaining the goals of national development. This booklet analyzes the regional and subregional trends, policies, and strategies in education.

Depending on the criteria of interest, a number of subregional groupings may be developed. In this study a typology of seven groups is identified and utilized to examine intraregional comparisons and to facilitate understanding of the range of education conditions and problems. The countries of South Asia, for example, contrast greatly with the more advanced East Asian economies on most economic, social, and educational indicators. The education policies and priorities of the latter may differ sharply from those of the former.

As part of the economic and social transformation taking place in Asia, education systems are expanding and being reoriented to cope with growth in social demand and to respond to economies driven by evolving industrial and information technologies. The Asian and Pacific region as a whole has made major advances in the quantitative and qualitative provision of education during the last few decades. Most DMCs have achieved, or are well on the way to achieving, universal primary education. For Southeast Asian countries basic education is increasingly being defined to include nine years of schooling. For many countries, the new thrusts are in expansion of secondary education; the coming decades will bring high rates of growth in tertiary education. Several East Asian economies currently have well-established mass systems of secondary and tertiary education. The more economically advanced are among the world's leaders in student achievement on core subject areas as measured by comparison of national test scores. In poorer countries and disadvantaged areas of the majority of countries, illiteracy persists and education opportunities remain limited and typically gender biased against girls. Changes in the locus of control over education are under way, being initiated, or subject to serious debate, in most Asian countries. The objectives of such reform vary by country and over time, but include the delegation of certain education responsibilities traditionally held in the central government to lower echelons. The extent of decentralization may have a profound effect on a broad range of planning, financial, curriculum, teaching, and evaluation decisions.

Although ADB and other international agencies may play significant roles, in meeting current social and education challenges in Asia, national and subnational governments remain the key actors. In recent years, government

71

efforts have been complemented to an increasing degree by private, community, and nongovernment actors. National, and in some countries local, governments are facing hard investment choices, often in the context of political uncertainty and with few resources for which there is much competition. Nevertheless, there is ample room for optimism. DMCs have demonstrated capacity for working within conditions of scarcity and uncertainty, for sharing information and knowledge regionally, and for valuing strong education institutions as requisites for attaining economic and social goals.

Note on the Author

Don Adams is Emeritus Professor in education policy studies at the University of Pittsburgh, United States. He is also an Honorary Fellow and former President of the Comparative and International Education Society (CIES). He is the author of many books, articles and monographs on international education, and a frequent consultant to international agencies in Asia. His books include *Education and Modernization in Asia* (1970), *Education in National Development* (1971), and *Education and Social Change in Korea* (with Esther Gottlieb, 1993). Address: 1106 Gilchrest Drive, Pittsburgh, PA 15235, United States. E-mail: dkadams@pitt.edu.

References

Asian Development Bank (ADB). 1991. *Education and Development in Asia and the Pacific.* Second edition. Manila: ADB.

————. 1997. *Emerging Asia: Changes and Challenges.* Manila: ADB.

Bray, M. 1996. *Counting the Full Cost: Parental and Community Financing of Education in East Asia.* Washington, DC: The World Bank in collaboration with UNICEF.

————. 1999. Control of Education: Issues and Tensions in Centralization and Decentralization. In *Comparative Education: The Dialectic of the Global and the Local,* edited by Arnove, R.F. and Torres, C.A. Lanham, Maryland: Rowman and Littlefield, 207-32.

————. 2000. *Community Partnerships in Education: Dimensions, Variations, and Implications.* Thematic Study for the World Forum on Education for All (EFA). Paris: EFA Secretariat, UNESCO.

————. 2002. *The Costs and Financing of Education: Trends and Policy Implications.* Series 'Education in Developing Asia'. Manila: ADB, and Hong Kong: Comparative Education Research Centre, University of Hong Kong.

Carnoy, M. 1995. Structural Adjustment and the Changing Face of Education. *International Labour Review* 134(6):653-73.

Chapman, D. 2002. *Management and Efficiency in Education: Goals and Strategies.* Series 'Education in Developing Asia'. Manila: ADB, and Hong Kong: Comparative Education Research Centre, University of Hong Kong.

Chapman, D., and Adams, D. 2002. *The Quality of Education: Dimensions and Strategies.* Series 'Education in Developing Asia'. Manila: ADB, and Hong Kong: Comparative Education Research Centre, University of Hong Kong.

Cheng, K.M. 1994. The Changing Legitimacy in a Decentralizing System: The State and Education Development in China. *International Journal of Educational Development* 14(3):265-69.

Haq, M. 1997. *Human Development in South Asia 1997.* Karachi: Oxford University Press.

Heyneman, S.P. 1997. Economic Growth and the International Trade in Education Reform. *Prospects* 27(4):501-30.

Jain, S.P., and Hochgesang, T.W., eds. 1995. *Emerging Trends in Panchayati Raj: Rural Local Self-Government in India.* New Delhi: National Institute of Rural Development.

Lee, W.O. 2002. *Equity and Access to Education: Themes, Tensions, and Policies.* Series 'Education in Developing Asia'. Manila: ADB, and Hong Kong: Comparative Education Research Centre, University of Hong Kong.

Lewin, K.M. 1996. *Access to Education in Emerging Asia: Trends, Challenges and Policy Options.* Manila: ADB.

Mahmood, N. 1997. *Trends, Issues and Policies. in Education: A Case Study of Pakistan.* Pakistan Institute of Development Economics. Country Sector Study prepared for ADB.

Manugue, E., Gonzalez, E.T., Laquian, A.C., Nadunop, M.F., Amar, M.C., and Valencia, S.D. 1997. *Policies, Trends and Issues in Philippine Education.* Development Academy of Philippines. Country Sector Study prepared for ADB.

Miroshnichenko, L., and Brimkulov, U. 1997. *Country Report: Regional Study of Trends, Issues and Policies in Education.* Kyrgyz Research Institute of Higher Education Problems, Ministry of Education, Science and Culture. Country Sector Study prepared for ADB.

Moegiadi. 1976. *Indonesia: Quality of Basic Education.* Jakarta: Balitbang Dikbud.

Muhammad, H. 1998. *The Relationship Between School Resources and Student Achievement in Indonesia.* Ph.D Dissertation. Pittsburgh, PA. University of Pittsburgh.

Murnane, R.J., and Cohen, D. 1986. Merit Pay and the Evaluation of the Problem: Why Some Merit Plans Fail and Few Survive. *Harvard Educational Review* 56(1):1-17.

Organisation for Economic Co-operation and Development (OECD). 1997. *Education at a Glance: OECD Indicators.* Paris: OECD.

Papua New Guinea, Institute of National Affairs. 1997. *Regional Study of Trends, Issues and Policies in Education: Papua New Guinea Country Case Study.* Country Sector Study prepared for ADB.

Postlethwaite, T.N., and Wiley, D., eds. 1992. *The IEA Study of Science II: Science Achievement in Twenty-three Countries.* Oxford: Pergamon.

Psacharopoulos, G. 1994. Returns to Investment in Education : A Global Update. *World Development* 22(9):1325-43.

Quibria, M.G., ed. 1994. *Rural Poverty in Developing Asia.* Vol. 1. Bangladesh, India and Sri Lanka. Manila: ADB.

Reimers, F. 1997. Changing Schools through Participatory Knowledge Management in El Salvador: Can Education Systems Learn? In *From Planning to Action: Government Initiatives for Improving School-Level Practice,* edited by D.W. Chapman, L.O. Mählck, and A.E.M. Smulders. Paris: UNESCO International Institute for Educational Planning, and Oxford: Pergamon.

Shaeffer, S. 1992. Collaborating for Educational Change: The Role of Parents and the Community in School Improvement. *International Journal of Educational Development* 12(4):277-95.

Shakya, B.R., Bajracharya, H.R., Thapa, J.B., and Chitrakar, R. 1998. *Trends, Issues and Policies of Education in Nepal: A Case Study.* Research Centre for Educational Innovation and Development, Tribhuvan University, Nepal. Country Sector Study prepared for ADB.

Suryadi, A. 1989. *Improving the Educational Quality of Primary Schools*. Jakarta: Balitbang Dikbud.

Tan, J.P., and Mingat, A. 1992. *Education in Asia: A Comparative Study of Cost and Financing*. Washington, DC: World Bank.

Tilak, J.B.G. 1994. *Education for Development in Asia*. New Delhi: Sage Publications.

————. 1997. The Effects of Adjustment on Education: A Review of Asian Experience. *Prospects* 27(1):85-107.

United Nations Development Programme (UNDP). 1990. *Human Development Report 1990*. New York: Oxford University Press for the United Nations Development Programme.

————. 1997. *Human Development Report 1997*. New York: Oxford University Press for the United Nations Development Programme.

————. 1999. *Human Development Report 1999*. New York: Oxford University Press for the United Nations Development Programme.

United Nations Educational, Scientific and Cultural Organization (UNESCO). 1989, 1993, 1996, 1998. *UNESCO Statistical Yearbook*. Paris: UNESCO.

UNESCO, Division of Statistics. 1999. *UNESCO Statistics*. Available: http://unescostat.unesco.org.

Viet Nam, National Institute for Educational Development. 1997. *Project: Regional Study of Trends, Issues and Policies in Education: Viet Nam Country Case Study*. Country Sector Study prepared for ADB.

Williams, J. 1997. Improving School-Community Relations in the Periphery. In *Quality Education for All*, edited by D. Nielsen and W.K. Cummings. New York: Garland.

Wirjomartono, S.H., Suryadi, A., Indriyanto, B., Purwadi, A., Cahyana, A., and Chamidi, S. 1997. *Study of Trends, Issues and Policies in Education: Indonesia Case Study*. Office of Educational and Cultural Research and Development, Indonesia. Country Sector Study prepared for ADB.

World Bank. 1995. *Priorities and Strategies for Education: A World Bank Review*. Washington, DC: World Bank.

————. 1996. *World Development Report 1996: From Plan to Market*. New York: Oxford University Press.

————. 1997. *World Development Report 1997: The State in a Changing World*. New York: Oxford University Press.

————. 1998. *World Development Report 1998/99: Knowledge for Development*. New York: Oxford University Press.

World Conference on Education for All (WCEFA). 1990. *World Declaration on Education for All*. New York: WCEFA Inter-Agency Commission.

Zhou, M. 1997. *Regional Studies of Trends, Issues and Policies in Education: Final Report of Country Case Study of the People's Republic of China*. National Center for Educational Development Research, the People's Republic of China. Country Sector Study prepared for ADB.

Appendix

The following is a list of the eight Country Sector Studies referred to in this booklet:

China, People's Republic of:
National Center for Education Development Research. 1997. *Regional Study of Trends, Issues and Policies in Education: Final Report of Country Case Study of the People's Republic of China.* Country Sector Study prepared for ADB.

Indonesia:
Office of Educational and Cultural Research and Development. 1997. *Study of Trends, Issues and Policies in Education (Indonesia Case Study).* Country Sector Study prepared for ADB. Members of the Research Team included: Sri Hardjoko Wirjomartono (Coordinator); Jiyono; Ace Suryadi; Jahja Umar; Jamil Ibrahim; Arief Sukadi; Suheru Muljoatmodjo; Bambang Indriyanto; Agung Purwadi; Ade Cahyana; Safrudin Chamidi

Kyrgyz Republic:
Kyrgyz Research Institute of Higher Education Problems, Ministry of Education, Science and Culture. Bishkek, Kyrgyz Republic. 1997. *Country Report: Regional Study of Trends, Issues and Policies in Education.* Country Sector Study prepared for ADB. Members of the Research Team included: D.A. Amanaliev; I.B. Becboev; G.M. Belaya; U.N. Brimkulov; N.N. Janaeva; M.T. Imankulova; L.P. Miroshnichenko; V.L. Machnovsky; S.K. Marzaev; A.A. Shaimergenov; V.K. Jantzen.

Nepal:
Research Centre for Educational Innovation and Development, Tribhuvan University. 1997. *Trends, Issues and Policies of Education in Nepal: A Case Study.* Tripureshwor, Kathmandu. Country Sector Study prepared for ADB. Members of the Research Team included: Hridaya Ratna Bajracharya; Bijaya Kumar Thapa; Roshan Chitrakar.

Pakistan:
Pakistan Institute of Development Economics. 1997. *Trends, Issues and Policies in Education: A Case Study of Pakistan.* Islamabad, Pakistan. Country Sector Study prepared for ADB. Researcher: Naushin Mahmood.

Papua New Guinea:

Institute of National Affairs. 1997. *Regional Study of Trends, Issues and Policies in Education: Papua New Guinea Country Case Study.* Country Sector Study prepared for ADB.

Philippines:

Development Academy of the Philippines. 1997. *Policies, Trends and Issues in Philippine Education.* A Case Study Commissioned by UNESCO-Bangkok, Thailand for ADB. The Task Force Members included: Ramon C. Bacani; Napoleon B. Imperial; Juan M. Sabulao; Mario Taguiwalo; Charles C. Villaneuva; Carmencita T. Abella; Alma Bella Z. Generao. Research Team Members included: Elizabeth Y. Manugue - Research Lead; Eduardo T. Gonzalez; Anicetas C. Laquian; Merialda F. Nadunop; Mercedita C. Amar; Shiela D. Valencia.

Viet Nam:

National Institute for Educational Development. 1997. *Regional Study of Trends, Issues and Policies in Education: Viet Nam Case Study.* Hanoi, Viet Nam. Country Sector Study prepared for ADB.

Index

Afghanistan, 3, 4, 5, 7, 12, 14, 16, 17, 18
age cohort, 6, 11, 12, 18
agriculture, 6, 21, 36, 61
  and education, 61
  employment, 8, 11, 17, 34
  GDP shares, 7, 8, 9
  labor force, 8, 16, 20, 34
  productivity, 11, 21, 37
Asian Development Bank (ADB), v, 2, 11, 15, 27, 33, 59, 65, 66, 67, 69, 71
Bangladesh, 4, 5, 7, 12, 14, 16, 18
basic education, v, 2, 8, 11, 15, 18, 21, 22, 23, 26, 33, 34–36, 37, 40, 43, 44, 49, 59, 60–62, 66, 71
Bhutan, 4, 5, 7, 12, 14, 16, 17, 19, 60
Cambodia, 4, 5, 7, 10, 12, 14, 16, 17
capitalism, 10
central government, 23, 39, 40, 43, 44, 48, 52, 56, 57, 71
centralization, 57
China, People's Republic of (PRC), 3, 7, 8, 10, 12, 14, 16, 27, 40, 48, 57, 60, 66, 67, 68
  coastal area, 21, 44
  decentralization, 42–45
  Ministry of Education, 43
  provincial government, 40, 43
  State Education Commission (SEdC), 43
citizenship skill, 34
civil society, 35
class size, 29
community, 23, 26, 31, 32, 33, 39, 40, 41, 43, 47, 48, 49, 51, 52, 53, 54, 57, 58, 61, 63, 67
consumerism, 23
Cook Islands, 4, 5, 14, 16, 17
cost-effective teaching, 33
curriculum, 15, 30, 32, 36, 38, 39, 41, 42, 43, 55, 58, 59, 61, 64, 71
decentralization, 2, 10, 33, 39–47, 48, 49, 50, 51, 52, 55, 56, 59, 71
dependency ratio, 6, 17, 20, 21, 22
distance education, 61

dropout, 9, 12, 17, 34, 52
early childhood education, 34
East Asia, 3, 6, 7, 8, 11, 22, 36, 63, 71
economic
  development, v
  growth, 1, 3, 6, 7, 8, 9, 11, 13, 16, 17, 20–24, 33, 34, 71
  productivity, 1, 11, 61
education
  attainment, 24
  development, 3, 17, 19, 34, 41
  expenditure, 13, 14, 15, 19, 23, 28, 29, 44, 60, 69
  governance, 2, 39, 40, 43, 45, 51, 52
  investment, v
  opportunities, 9, 23, 44, 57, 60, 71
  policy, 10, 28, 56, 64, 65
  trends, 1, 2, 13, 20, 65
effective schooling, 31
elitism, 26
employment, 6, 7, 8, 11, 15, 24, 25, 34, 36, 38, 60, 62
enrollment rate, 17, 18, 23, 34. *See* also Gross Enrollment Rate (GER)
equity, 23, 24, 25, 27, 33, 38, 43, 44, 58, 59, 60, 61
fertility rate, 3, 5, 6, 17, 21
Fiji Islands, 4, 5, 7, 12, 14, 16, 17
first-level education, 9, 12, 13, 17. See also basic education, primary education
gender, 8, 10, 18, 24, 25, 26, 30, 61
Gender-related Development Index (GDI), 6, 8
globalization, 22, 25
Grama Swaraj, 45
Gross Domestic Product (GDP) per capita, 3, 7, 9, 16, 17, 20, 21
Gross Enrollment Rate (GER), 9, 12, 16, 17
gross national product (GNP), 17
higher education, 10, 23, 26, 33, 37, 38, 44, 59, 62, 63, 64. *See* also

tertiary education, third-level
    education
Hong Kong, China, 3, 4, 5, 7, 10, 12,
    14, 16, 17, 21, 27, 30
human capital, 8, 11, 20, 21, 22, 24, 26
Human Development Index (HDI), 6, 7,
    8, 15, 16, 17
Human Poverty Index (HPI), 6, 8
human rights, 25
illiteracy rate, 7, 8, 9, 17, 18. *See* also
    literacy rate
India, 4, 5, 7, 9, 10, 12, 14, 16, 18, 29,
    30, 40, 48, 57, 60
    decentralization, 45–47
    Department of Education, 46
    Ministry of Human Resource
        Development, 46
Indonesia, 4, 5, 6, 7, 8, 12, 13, 14, 16,
    17, 28, 29, 30, 40, 60, 66
industrialization, 6, 23, 25, 61, 63
input-output model, 27
instructional materials, 29, 61
international assistance, 66–70
International Association for the
    Evaluation of Educational
    Achievement (IEA), 27
Kazakhstan, 4, 5, 7, 12, 13, 14, 16, 17,
    18, 19
Kiribati, 4, 5, 7, 14, 16, 17, 19
Korea, Republic of, 4, 5, 7, 8, 10, 12,
    14, 16, 17, 18, 22, 23, 27, 30
Kyrgyz Republic, 4, 5, 7, 12, 13, 14,
    16, 17, 19, 41, 66
labor market, 6, 11, 21, 24, 36
Lao People's Democratic Republc (Lao
    PDR), 4, 5, 7, 10, 12, 14, 16, 17, 19
literacy rate, 3, 9, 14, 17, 18. *See* also
    illiteracy rate
localization, 39–47
Malaysia, 4, 5, 7, 8, 12, 14, 16, 17, 18,
    29, 30
Maldives, 3, 4, 5, 7, 12, 14, 16, 17, 18,
    19
market economies, 20, 44
Marshall Islands, 3, 4, 5, 7, 16, 21
Micronesia, 4, 5, 7, 16
mid-year population, 18
mobilization, 42, 43, 49, 51, 53
Mongolia, 4, 5, 7, 10, 12, 14, 16, 17
mortality rate, 3, 5, 6, 17
Myanmar, 4, 5, 7, 12, 14, 16, 17
Nauru, 4, 5, 16

Nepal, 3, 4, 5, 7, 8, 12, 14, 15, 16, 17,
    18, 19, 24, 30, 41, 60, 66, 67
    Central Bureau of Statistics, 16
    District Education Office, 41
    Ministry of Education, 16, 41, 67
    National Planning Commission, 16
    Regional Education Directorate
        (RED), 41
    School Management Committee, 41
nongovernment organization (NGO),
    10, 53, 57, 66
Organisation for Economic Co-
    operation and Development
    (OECD), 65
Pacific DMCs, 48
Pakistan, 4, 5, 7, 8, 9, 12, 14, 16, 17,
    18, 49, 57, 60, 66, 67, 69, 70
    Ministry of Education, 41
Papua New Guinea (PNG), 9, 12, 16,
    17, 18, 27, 48, 66, 67, 68, 69, 70
    provincial government, 49
partnership, 35, 57
    central-local, 50, 52
    government levels, 49
    public-private, 33
    with Asian Development Bank
        (ADB), 59, 70
Philippines, 4, 5, 7, 8, 10, 12, 13, 14,
    16, 17, 24, 27, 29, 30, 34, 35, 41,
    60, 66, 67, 68, 69
poverty, 1, 6, 7, 8, 9, 11, 20, 21, 24–
    25, 66
preprimary education, 30, 34
primary education, 10, 12, 15, 18, 22,
    23, 34, 35, 41, 42, 43, 45, 46, 47,
    62, 63, 71. *See* also basic
    education, first-level education
purchasing power parity (PPP) dollars,
    7, 8
repeaters, 12, 18. *See* also repetition
repetition, 9, 17, 30. *See* also
    repeaters
rural region, 9, 11, 26, 28, 34, 43, 45,
    48, 60, 62, 66
Samoa, 4, 5, 16, 17, 48
scholarship, 46, 61, 64
school management, 32, 54, 58, 61
secondary education, 2, 10, 13, 15, 17,
    21, 23, 26, 33, 34, 36–37, 60, 62–
    63, 71. See also second-level
    education
second-level education, 9, 12. *See* also
    secondary education

Singapore, 3, 4, 5, 7, 8, 10, 12, 14, 16,
    17, 18, 27
social
    change, 1, 3, 9–11, 23, 25–27, 55
    cohesion, 25–27
    equality, 26
    justice, 25
    mobility, 27, 60
    opportunity, 26
Solomon Islands, 4, 5, 7, 14, 17
South Asia, 3, 6, 8, 9, 22
Southeast Asia, 7, 22, 63, 71
Sri Lanka, 4, 5, 7, 11, 12, 14, 16, 17
Taipei,China, 4, 5, 8, 10, 14, 16, 17,
    22, 27
teacher training
    in-service, 28, 30, 32, 34, 41
    preservice, 28, 29
technical education, 33, 34. *See* also
    vocational education
tertiary education, 2, 17, 60, 62, 63–64,
    71. *See* also higher education, third-
    level education
Thailand, 4, 5, 7, 8, 10, 11, 12, 14, 16,
    17, 27, 29, 30, 48
third-level education, 9, 12. *See* also
    higher education, tertiary education

Tonga, 4, 5, 7, 14, 16, 17
Tuvalu, 4, 5, 14, 16, 17
United Nations Children's Fund
    (UNICEF), 57
United Nations Development
    Programme (UNDP), 21
United Nations Educational, Scientific
    and Cultural Organization
    (UNESCO), 13, 57, 65
urban
    areas, 3, 6, 11, 32, 34, 63
    population, 4, 6, 10, 11, 17
urbanization, 6
Uzbekistan, 4, 5, 7, 12, 13, 14, 16, 17,
    18
Vanuatu, 4, 5, 7, 12, 14, 16, 17, 18
Viet Nam, 4, 5, 7, 10, 12, 14, 16, 17,
    66, 67
    Ministry of Education, 42
village education, 41, 43, 47, 49
vocational education, 34, 63. *See* also
    technical education
vocationalization, 36
World Bank, The, 11, 22, 27, 33, 65, 68
World Declaration on Education for All,
    50